MY STRANGE WORLD

STEVE STOCKTON

BEYOND THE FRAY
Publishing

Copyright © 2015, 2020 Steve Stockton
Published by: Beyond The Fray Publishing, a division of Beyond The Fray, LLC

This book or any portion thereof may not be reproduced or used in any manner whatsoever without the express written permission of the publisher except for the use of brief quotations in a book review. All rights reserved.

First edition: 2015 by Steve Stockton
Second edition: 2020 by Beyond The Fray Publishing

ISBN 13: 978-1-7344198-2-5

Beyond The Fray Publishing, a division of Beyond The Fray, LLC, San Diego, CA
www.beyondthefraypublishing.com

BEYOND THE FRAY

Publishing

INTRODUCTION

I've always had an interest in the paranormal, although it might be safer to say that the paranormal has always had an interest in *me*. I feel that the "great unknown" sought me out first, and I repaid the favor in turn. From my first sighting of an apparition at age six, to a haunted house I've lived in recently—one of many, I might add—these are my stories.

In 2013, I published a book of other people's true, weird encounters called *Strange Things in the Woods*. These were stories that I had collected since childhood from the spectrum of immediate family, distant family, and family friends. The subsequent volumes have included stories from a wider circle of friends, acquaintances and even those who read the first book and/or listened to one of my many appearances on radio broadcasts as well as podcasts. Throughout it all, I would often have show hosts or interested readers ask me about *my* experiences. I would usually demur or offer a condensed version of an experience—but it finally dawned on me that I did, indeed, have enough experiences to fill a book. When I first began writing them down, I felt as reluctant as some of the storytellers in my first volume. However, just like they did, the more I began to write, the easier the writing came, and I had to eventually agree that, yes, these would make for an enjoyable read.

So here lie my personal stories, warts and all, of my experiences with the paranormal, the bizarre and the unknown. While you won't find anything in here as wild as, say, the Amityville Horror, the Dover Demon, the Flatwoods Monster, Mothman or Nessie, there are some unexplained encounters that have shaped my outlook and beliefs.

I would like to thank all those who encouraged me along the way, including my family, friends and fellow paranormal enthusiasts—I dedicate this book to you.

—Steve
Portland, OR
August 2015

CHAPTER ONE

MY FIRST GHOST

[I thought I'd open the book with this story, since not only was it my first paranormal experience, but also my first sighting of a full-body apparition. This happened in the Solway community of west Knox County in East Tennessee, just across Melton Hill Lake from the "Atomic City" of Oak Ridge. If you've heard any of my radio or podcast appearances, you've probably heard a condensed version of this story... I present it here in its entirety for the first time in print.]

The first ghost I can remember seeing was when I was a small child. I say the first I "remember" because I had other strange experiences as an even smaller child, but unfortunately do not remember a lot of those details.

In the summer of 1969, my mother and father and I lived in a brick rancher-style house, which my father had contracted to be built in 1964. Also that summer, a new house was built on the property adjoining ours, and the occupants had a son (I'll call him John) who was a year younger than myself. I was overjoyed at having someone next door to play with (although, since this was in the country, "next door" was actually several hundred yards away, with an old growth of dark woods between our houses).

John and I became best friends and had already made plans to go trick-or-treating in the fall. We played together every day when I got home from school. I was in first grade, and back at this time the area in which we lived in Tennessee did not have a state/county kindergarten, and as such it wasn't required by law. I had gone to a private church-run kindergarten the year before, but John's parents elected not to send him to kindergarten, so he was always home during the day.

This particular day, I'm assuming it was the early part of September, as I had been to school that day and John and I, as I stated above, had already made plans for Halloween. So, as near as I can remember, this happened sometime in September or early October.

I had walked over to John's house, but his father told me he had gone to the grocery store with his mom and would be back soon. I walked back home and began playing in my own front yard while waiting for John to return. Since our street was a dead end into the lake with only one way in or out past our house, I would be able to see their car when John and his mom returned.

Being out in the country (in what was then a semi-rural area), our house sat quite a ways back from the paved road. In fact, our gravel driveway measured exactly 212 feet from our garage door to the paved street. I eventually measured this out using a surveyor's tape when I was older and holding bicycle sprint races from the garage to the road and back.

Our yard had originally been a rough, wooded area, but had been cleared off before the house was built. At the time of this incident, it was mostly old-growth pine trees and a rolling landscape of small hills and trenches, which my father had sown with meadow grass. It was a boy's dream of a place to play—just enough trees to make it interesting, and enough dips and hills to provide for exciting "off-road" bicycling (this was in a time prior to the popularity of mountain biking or even BMX, but I am here to tell you that my Schwinn Sting Ray was a ferocious beast in the dirt as well as a speed demon on the asphalt).

Off to the sides of our yard, there was heavy undergrowth and dark, spooky woods to explore. Our property consisted of about twenty or so acres, with less than five even partially cleared. For small boys like we were, full of life and fun and adventure, the bucolic countryish setting provided for an idyllic childhood.

On this early fall day, I busied myself awaiting the return of my new friend. I was a little over halfway into the yard from the house, so it was a distance of ninety yards. I was well beyond the pines that shaded our house, and I had a very clear line of sight—I made sure of it so I could watch the inverted T intersection, which was right in front of our property. Since the road we lived on dead-ended into the lake, past this intersection, there was only one way in or out—at the intersection, of course, there was two ways in and out, and I had a perfect vantage point to view both—I would not miss the return of my friend regardless of which road his mom drove in on.

Shortly, I'd guess it was fifteen minutes or so that I had been quietly surveilling the road, I watched in anticipation as a car came down the hill, in the center of the inverted T where there was a STOP sign. As the car rolled downhill to the intersection and came to a stop, I had already begun to walk toward the road, as I believed it was John and his mom returning. Suddenly, without warning or with any doors opening on the car, I observed a small child run from behind the car and then dart across directly in front of it. I knew immediately that it was not my five-year-old friend, but rather a toddler, maybe only a year or so old. My first thought was that the child was going to be run over, because the driver wouldn't be able to see something so small directly in front of the car.

As it turned out, the driver was not only NOT John's mom, but a male I didn't recognize—I hadn't seen him before and never saw him after in the nine plus years we continued to live at this address. Furthermore, as I observed the child run across the road at a catty-corner angle, the driver didn't register that he had seen the child at all—he looked both ways and then lackadaisically turned toward the direction that dead-ended in the lake a mile or so away.

The child was so young, he seemed unable to control his speed. If you've ever observed a child that hasn't mastered mere walking, but breaks into a run—then you understand what I'm saying about control. Unable to stop, most kids will lose control completely and fall down. Well, this was exactly what this small child did, but by the time he fell, he had crossed all the way across the road and into our yard—and when he fell, he disappeared. As strange as that sounds, that was exactly what happened—he ran across the street (unobserved by the driver in the car), crossed into our yard maybe ten feet or so, and fell down—and when he hit the ground, he simply no longer existed. Never taking my eyes off it, I walked directly to the spot where the child disappeared.

In my mind's eye, I can still see the little boy as plain as day—he was about a year and a half old, was fair-skinned and had sandy blond hair. He was wearing a pair of blue shorts with matching suspenders and a small blue ball cap. His short-sleeved, button-up shirt was white, as were his socks and shoes. When I arrived at the spot where he vanished, I expected to see a child in a hole of some sort in our yard that I had inexplicably missed. (I doubted this theory as soon as it popped into my head, as I knew every inch of the yard that had been cleared, as well as a majority of that which was still wooded.) However, when I arrived at the very spot (I suspect it took me all of ten seconds), there was nothing to be found—no small child in blue, no hole, nothing I could have mistaken for a child who ran across the road and fell down—absolutely nothing.

Even at the tender age of six, I admit I was stymied. I wasn't scared, not in the least, but I was very puzzled. I was smart enough to know that I had just witnessed something that wasn't supposed to happen—little boys dressed in blue do not run across the street and fall down in yards only to disappear. I walked the area several times over, tracing and retracing my steps. I even tried convincing myself I had imagined the whole ordeal, yet I knew better—I knew just as well then in 1969 as I do now in 2015 as to what I observed. Surprisingly, I never mentioned it to my parents until I was well into adulthood. My dad's response was "Huh. Wonder what it was?" and my mother's equally cryptic response, "There were a lot of strange things that happened when we lived down there." Sadly, she never elaborated, and I'm unsure if I knew of all the "strangeness" she spoke of, although I did know (and experience) what I'm sure was more than my share.

To this day, I don't know if there is any "meaning" to what I saw—that was kind of my grandma's deal, anyway (my maternal grandma, the gypsy witch—you'll meet her in a subsequent chapter)—everything that wasn't readily explainable had some esoteric, hidden meaning. Although in her case it was usually an omen, a portent, a foretelling of something bad surely on the way. Fortunately, as far as I know, no little fair-skinned kids perished in the general vicinity, and other than a few failed relationships, I've survived an additional forty-five years on the planet since the incident with no ill effects, plagues, curses, tragedies or swarms of locusts. I've only had a couple of close calls in car accidents (neither one my fault), I've never been arrested (never had more than a traffic ticket), and still have a head full of hair (although I do have some gray—but, as my dad used to say, "I'd rather have it turn gray than turn loose"). Sorry, Granny!

I think if there was a meaning to the experience, it was just the supernatural world around me kind of letting me know "hey, you're different, and you might see some things that don't make a lot of sense, but don't get all carried away about it..." Looking back, it seemed more like what I've come to know as a residual haunting rather than an active one, although I was unable through any research to find any child that had been killed at that intersection, in forever. This is also not too far from the area where, when my brother was about three or four years old, he observed *himself* place a Bible in his red Radio Flyer wagon and pull it up a hill. His child-self felt compelled to do exactly the same as he had observed his doppelgänger doing. About twenty-four years later, he felt the call to preach, and has since pastored several churches and founded several ministries over the last forty years. He feels his initial experience was an earlier foretelling of what he would become in life, and in his case, it was accurate.

If any of my readers have had a similar experience, or feel that they might be able to provide any insight into the experience I had, I'd be more than happy to discuss it with you. I'm open to any and all theories, and my contact information, as always, can be found at the end of this volume.

CHAPTER TWO

MARSHALL SAYS GOODBYE

In the early 1980s, I worked for a large grocery chain in the South, which was owned by the Kroger Co. out of Cincinnati, Ohio. I was not quite out of my teens yet and rather enjoyed working in the store's deli department. I had friends who worked at the same location who held positions such as courtesy clerk and cashier, but I felt that my deli position was easier, less stressful, and I made the same pay as my friends—yet I never had to deal with bringing shopping carts in from the parking lot or getting yelled at by a customer regarding an improperly priced item. For a teenager, it was a sweet gig.

While working in the deli, one of my co-workers was an older divorced lady who had made her way to Tennessee from California with her two young sons in tow. As it can sometimes be difficult to be a single mom raising two rowdy boys, she always seemed to have her hands full and thus wasn't always able to concentrate on her work. One day, when I was recounting some of my teenage skateboarding escapades, she asked me if I would —for pay—hang out with her sons and try to help them stay out of trouble. Her oldest son (I'll call him Marshall, and his younger brother, Mikey) also enjoyed skateboarding, so she was sure we'd hit it off, despite an age difference of a few years. As near as I can recall, Marshall was fourteen at the time, and Mikey would have been about ten.

I readily agreed, except I refused to accept any payment. I knew the frustration that could come from being an outcast, of being a loner-ish skateboarder with a weird haircut and an odd taste in music. I was sure Marshall and I would have a blast, and Mikey would enjoy being allowed to tag along on our skate treks. The next day at work, she told me the boys were both thrilled at the prospect, and we made arrangements for me to come over to her apartment on our next days off at the same time.

A few days later, I went over and met her kids. They turned out to be a couple of charming little guys who only seemed to give their mom guff or get into trouble when they were bored. Over the next year or so, I took the boys skating with me on many occasions, and we became fast friends. The two even begged me to marry their mother so I could become their "dad," but were understanding when informed that while I felt no romantic inclinations toward their middle-aged mother

(I had my eye on a raven-haired, blue-eyed courtesy clerk who, like me, was out of high school but not quite out of her teens, and also shared my musical interests), but we could always be friends.

Over the next couple of years, I grew very close to both boys, but particularly Marshall. He was like the little brother I had always begged for as a child. We skated all over the area, both becoming quite good. Marshall and I both also shared a penchant for filmmaking and made a lot of horror and comedy shorts using a giant shoulder-mount video camera and portable VTR unit I had acquired somewhere in my travels.

Around this time, I became enamored with a clerk at a local video store (remember those? I mean video stores, not clerks, but they do kind of go hand in hand…) and began seeing her regularly, eventually moving in together in a lovely garden apartment on the west side of Oak Ridge. Marshall was kind of crestfallen at my new life, and although he would often come over to visit and just hang out, I'm sure he felt like the proverbial third wheel. In the interim, his mother had also started dating and was planning to marry a gentleman she'd met at work. Marshall said he felt like a lost ball in high weeds. My girlfriend and I made plans to include him in more of our activities and even had designs on "fixing him up" with one of her single female friends.

One Friday night, my girlfriend and I were returning to the apartment we now shared, after a Chinese dinner at Oak Ridge Marina. I distinctly remember her remarking how incredibly dark it seemed out that night, which I chalked up to her getting the heebie-jeebies from the horror film we'd taken in earlier that night. We went home and went to bed.

I awoke the next morning to something strange. A pair of LA Gear tennis shoes that I rarely wore anymore and kept buried in the closet were shoved right up next to the mattress (we didn't have a bed at the time, just a mattress on the floor), my face almost in them. Inside the right shoe was an unopened pack of Kool Menthol Lights cigarettes, a brand I hadn't smoked in a long time. While puzzling over how this came to be and pointing it out to my still-sleepy girlfriend, we were interrupted by the ringing of the telephone. My girlfriend walked into the living room and answered it, with me following behind. Without saying a word and white as a sheet, she turned and handed me the handset.

It was Marshall's mother, and she tearfully informed me that Marshall had been killed the previous night or early that morning, sometime around midnight. Tragically, he had snuck out of his mother's apartment and had gone for a late night skate session, alone. He was skating on the shoulder of the road, but a sixteen-year-old who had just received her driver's license the week prior took the curve a little too fast in her father's BMW and had plowed into Marshall. He crashed through the windshield of the car and, mercifully, was thought to have died instantly on impact. The teenaged driver of the car was more concerned about what her father was going to say about his destroyed sports car than the fact that she had snuffed out a young life.

Marshall's mom said something about contacting me later regarding funeral arrangements, but I was too numb and devastated for any of it to register clearly. Sobbing heavily, I returned to the bedroom and flopped back down on the mattress, letting my emotions flow. Later, after I began to calm down, I looked over the edge of the bed and once again spied the pack of cigarettes—and then it hit me like a ton of bricks.

Marshall's mom, being from California, was somewhat lenient with her parenting. A smoker herself, she had allowed Marshall to smoke—provided he could pay for his own cigarettes. He would often bum change off of me and have his mom pick up a pack for him at the convenience store across the street from their apartment complex. His preferred brand? Kool Menthol Lights. I shuddered despite the growing heat in the small apartment.

To this day, I feel that the shoes were shoved in my face to get my attention—something Marshall, always the prankster, would totally have done and then laughed heartily about it later. And the cigarettes were a gift, a way of saying goodbye to a friend. I put off smoking them for a long time, but I finally broke down and consumed them, feeling that it's what Marshall would have wanted. After the pack was gone, I had a more peaceful feeling about him.

Coincidentally, I had often sat in on Ouija board sessions with Marshall's mom and her sister. The pair seemed to have a talent for the talking oracle and had the ability to answer questions that they would have had no earthly way of knowing the answers. However, after Marshall's tragic death, I was informed by the aunt that his mom was no longer able to use the Ouija... It seems that every time she attempted to contact the other side, a very strong entity claiming to be Marshall would connect itself to the board and refuse to leave.

CHAPTER THREE

THE GHOST KITTENS

[Are there such things as animal ghosts or spirits? I'm inclined to believe so, not only due to other encounters I've heard and/or read about, but also from personal experience. In volume one of my Strange Things in the Woods series (Lucky Secret Press, Bangor, Maine 2013), I wrote about ghost kittens heard along a creek bank—but in my own personal experience, I heard them beneath the floorboards of my bedroom, from childhood to my mid-teenage years.]

Growing up, I lived in a brick rancher-style house, built new when I was but a few months old. Needless to say, we were the first family to live in the house. My father had worked closely with the builder, and the house was built to exacting specifications. Rather than have a basement, my father preferred an unfinished crawlspace underneath the house. And I'm here to tell you, it was just that—you had exactly enough room to crawl. The only way you could have stood is if you were a toddler. Every few feet, there were iron grates with one-inch squares, and a wire screen mesh behind that. The only thing that could enter was fresh air when the louvers were open.

One day while playing in my bedroom (which had a hardwood floor with an area rug), I became tired and rested my head on the carpet—only to be surprised by the sound of several tiny kittens mewling! Shocked, I immediately got together some gear (namely, a flashlight) and headed into the crawlspace to rescue the kittens.

The crawlspace ran the entire length of the three-bedroom house, only ending where the concrete pad for our single-car garage was attached. There was only one way in our out—a small two-foot-by-three-foot door on the high side of the house. My father stored lawn care instruments and tools in the tallest part of the space, so the door was always padlocked from the outside. The tiny louvered openings (there were four total, two on the front and a matching equidistant pair on the back side of the dwelling) were approximately one-inch metal grid, with a fine mesh (think window screen) securely fastened over that. Only the tiniest of insects could have penetrated that, and there was no way a cat or kitten of any size could gain entry of its own doing or volition.

I located the key from the cabinet in the garage where it always hung from a hook and, with trusty giant flashlight in hand, set out to enter the netherworld of the crawlspace. Previously, I had remained content to peer in when my father was putting something in or taking something out—the crawlspace was dark, dank and seemed to be a haven for spiders—not my idea of fun at the time.

As expected, I found the lock firmly in place on the hasp screwed into the crawlspace door. If anyone had been in, they would have had to have taken the time to unscrew the hasp and then reattach same. As the painted wooden door creaked open, I thumbed the button on my flashlight and flooded the darkened crawlspace with light.

The only things near the opening were the gardening and lawn implements my father normally stored in the space. Kneeling, I played the flashlight beam over the area, peering into the far corners as well as I could. If possible, I wanted to rescue the cat and her kittens without going underneath the house. It's not that I was scared of the dark (actually, far from it) and I wasn't really keen on the spider inhabitants, but my real fear was one of the neighborhood pranksters would lock me inside the crawlspace. I considered this for a bit, then smugly put the padlock into the pocket of my jeans and crawled inside.

Regardless of the creepy factor, I gently closed the plywood door behind me, plunging the crawlspace into absolute darkness. Armed with the somewhat narrow and not-so-bright beam of my flashlight, I began the hunched over "crab walk" to scour the part of the crawlspace with the most headroom. As I made my way farther back, I actually had to lie on my belly in the musty, dusty dirt and "Indian crawl" my way back towards where the crawlspace ended and the concrete pad of the garage floor began.

When I was finished, I had covered every inch of the blasted crawlspace—and there were absolutely no kittens to be found. No trace of anything except for a few annoyed spiders (which were as happy to be left alone as I was to leave them alone), there were no other living creatures within these dirt, cinderblock, brick and wood confines. Rather perplexed (and somewhat disappointed—I wanted pet kittens!), I made my way back to the wooden door and sighed in relief when it opened, bathing me in a shaft of sunlight and a puff of fresh air—no local yokel prankster had spotted my vulnerable quest and decided to lock me in. I climbed out of the opening, brushed the dirt from my clothes and cobwebs from my hair, and headed back inside to think this turn of events over.

As if to tempt fate, I marched straight into my bedroom in the back southwest corner of the house and flopped down on my area rug exactly as before. Sure enough, within the space of fifteen odd minutes, I once again heard the unmistakable mewling of at least two or three kittens. I tried to ignore the sound as best I could, but eventually it got the best of me. I geared up once again and headed back into the crawlspace, determined to put an end to this once and for all.

As I sort of expected, the second trip was the same. As well as subsequent third and fourth trips, eventually totaling at least a dozen, I'm sure. The kittens started their eerie meow and mewling when I was approximately ten years old, and continued on for some time. Although, for whatever reason (perhaps old age?) my parents were never able to hear the kittens, no matter how determined they were. However, my best friend and next-door neighbor, "John," visited often, and he could hear the kittens as well—imagine my shock and surprise the first time he quipped, "Hey, I think you have kittens under your house," when I had never mentioned my previous experiences.

The last time I heard the kittens was when I was fifteen years old. We were moving to a new house in the Karns area, and my bed and furniture had already been moved. As I fell asleep on the floor during the last night I would ever sleep in the house, I drifted off, tired from the day's activities, with the sound of mewling phantom kittens in my ear.

In my second book, *More Strange Things in the Woods*, I wrote about a ghostly dog, who, even though he had passed away, continued to be sighted on the family farm. In fact, there are a lot of such tales. I have also heard of cats, long since buried in the back yard, that would brush against their owner's ankle in the dark, or perhaps take a contented rest on the bed in the dark, purring all the while. If you have a ghostly pet story to tell, I'd love to hear it. Feel free to contact me via any of the means found at the end of this book.

CHAPTER FOUR

THE THING IN THE DITCH

[To this day, I still have no idea what this "thing" was that I encountered—not once, but several times and spaced out over several years. Certainly as a child—but also as a young adult—this is one of the few encounters I've had that actually scared me—and I mean to the point of being scared out of my mind.

If you've ever listened to any of my numerous radio interviews, you'll know that it takes a lot (and I mean A LOT) to truly frighten me—I saw a full-bodied apparition at the tender age of six (see chapter one) and was more intrigued than frightened. But the frightening thing about this set of encounters wasn't what I saw, but rather what I couldn't see—and I think that is the sole circumstance that made the encounter so inherently scary.]

  I don't remember what we were doing at the time, but I remember the location extremely well. I was playing in the edge of the woods, near an ancient ditch line on my parents' property, there was an old wire structure nearby, I think it had been a dog run at one time, where my brother had kept hunting dogs before I was born. I was just poking around, looking at nothing in particular. It was summertime, school was out, and I was kind of bored. When you were a kid living out in the rural wilds of East Tennessee, you had to make your own fun. I wouldn't be bored for very much longer, however.

I had just left the crumbling, rusted ruins of the wire dog enclosure and walked nearer to the edge of the ditch. The ditch itself was probably eight feet deep and a good thirty feet across. Suddenly, the forest seemed off. Everything seemed too quiet, like being in a vacuum. I stood still, trying to figure out what was going on. I glanced up toward the crest of the small hill, just before it dropped into the ditch—and then all hell broke loose.

Looking back, the only way I can describe it is that it looked like some large animal was running toward me, kicking up leaves in its wake—the truly frightening part being that whatever was kicking leaves a foot into the air was completely invisible.

I did what any kid of seven years old would have done —the instant the paralysis of fear broke, I ran down the hill toward home, screaming like a maniac. I was making so much noise that my mother heard me coming down the hill and was actually waiting for me on the back porch when I arrived. I was out of breath, a shaking, sobbing mess. It was several minutes before I could gather myself and calm down enough to answer all the questions my now-distraught mother was firing at me. I tried my best to explain what I had witnessed—and what

I HADN'T seen—that was the part that scared me the most. She held me close and took me inside the house to further help me calm down and stay that way, for as soon as I would start recounting the tale, I would once again begin to panic—that's how truly frightened I was. She promised we'd sort it all out as soon as my father got home, and she even called my brother and asked him to stop by after work.

When my father came home, my brother arrived about the same time. I was still somewhat shaken, and my mother did her best to explain what had happened. I accompanied my father and brother outside and almost to the area where the "attack" had occurred. There was no way I was willing to go all the way back to the top side of the ditch where the thing had begun chasing me. Although they could clearly see where the leaves had been disturbed just as I had described, like an adult running and kicking up leaves as far and as high as possible, there wasn't a sign of anything else. After conjecturing about the possibility of several different animals (both wild and domestic), I dutifully eliminated each one, because those were all things you could *see*. Both my father and brother both concluded that they had no idea what I had witnessed chasing me. They believed me, due to the fact that I wouldn't have been able to fake being scared that genuinely and also because they had both had their own inexplicable encounters in the woods on other occasions.

I shied away from that part of the ditch, but, oddly enough, had no problems playing in or near it several hundred yards farther down. On the rare occasions when

I did visit the part where I'd had my encounter, I made sure I wasn't alone. A couple of times, I even enlisted the help of my best friend, John, sort of using each other for bait—one would stand near where I had the encounter while the other hid a short distance down the hill behind a tree. It didn't work. Whatever had chased me was smarter than we had given it credit for, a fact that really didn't surprise me in the least.

I sort of forgot about the encounter ("ignored" is probably a more descriptive word) and just stayed away from the upper portion of the ditch line when alone. Other than the occasional "What do you think that was that scared you by the ditch?" from my father, I didn't think much about it after the initial nightmares faded into the mists of time.

Flash forward eight years. I'm fifteen years old now, a much more accomplished woodsman, and it takes a lot to scare me. We had sold the property where I grew up and were preparing to move to a new split-level house we'd had custom built a few miles away in the Karns community of west Knox County, where I attended high school.

I'd spent the last few days wistfully exploring my childhood haunts one last time, knowing I would, perhaps, never again be able to visit under the same circumstance. I was sort of laughing to myself as I walked up to the area of the ditch, remembering the sheer terror I had experienced as a child. At the time, the eight years that had passed seemed like a lifetime—and in a way, I guess they were.

I mounted the top edge of the ditch and peered down inside, wondering what on earth I had witnessed all those years ago—when I heard a familiar noise. The sound of running in the leaves! I looked down into the ditch and saw the exact same circumstance I had witnessed years before. The leaves were being kicked to and fro by something headed straight for me. I moved away from the ditch and started down the hill, not quite running yet. When whatever "it" was came out of the ditch and continued speeding toward me in the leaves, I broke into a run. At least I didn't scream and cry this time. That was my last visit to the ditch. We moved into our new house about a month later.

A few years after, I was at a party with a friend in west Knoxville. It was one of those parties where I only knew the person I was with, and didn't know anyone else at the party. A few of the girls in attendance had found a Ouija board behind the host of the party's sofa and had received her (somewhat reluctant) permission to play with it. If memory serves correctly, there were four girls working the board while the rest of the room was encouraged to ask questions. When it came my turn to ask the mystifying oracle a question, I had a doozie.

"What scared me when I was a child?" I asked, offering no additional information whatsoever in regard to the incident to which I was referring. Slowly, the planchette began to move across the board, which spelled two words: W-A-T-E-R S-P-R-I-T-E. When the Ouija group looked to me for an explanation, I merely smiled and shrugged. The next day I went to the library (for this was at least a decade prior to the advent of the internet) and looked up everything I could find regarding "water sprites" or "water spirits." It turns out they are a mythological entity, an elemental earth spirit, if you will.

These "water guardians," also known as "Naiads," are said to be found around streams. This incident happened not more than a hundred yards from an area where no less than seven natural springs flow out of a hillside and combine into one, then flow into the nearby lake. Had I chanced upon some strange place that was sacred to the fae or fairy folk? If so, how come no one else was chased away by the sprite? Was it because of my sensitivity to all things paranormal (bear in mind that the first incident at the ditch took place only a little more than a year after my experience with the ghost toddler that opens this book). The mind boggles.

Another theory I've entertained is due to the ditch having been the road through the area some decades prior. Was the ghost of a murdered Revolutionary War or Civil War soldier doomed to protect an area near the stream over and over for the rest of eternity? A few years prior, my father and brother had found a broken Civil War era bayonet near the creek while clearing brush, and East Tennessee is known to be dotted with sites of smaller skirmishes in addition to some of the larger battles.

Yet a third theory surfaced while talking to a family friend, who was a bona fide treasure hunter. He claimed that he had heard tales of a treasure buried in the Solway area going back before the Civil War. He also related tales of strange happenings when he did find hidden treasure (see the story "The Rusted Tractor" in my second book, *More Strange Things in the Woods*). Sort of like the way pirates were said to kill a crew mate at the site of a buried treasure, in order for his spirit to forever protect the buried loot.

In the end, I have no explanation—particularly not a rational one. I only know that this pair of encounters are among the most frightening I have ever had. As always, I engage my readers to provide me with possible explanations or theories.

CHAPTER FIVE

THE BEAST OF SWANSON LANE

[In this chapter, I'll recount what I not-so-lovingly refer to as "the Beast of Swanson Lane"—which is one of the more frightening encounters with the unknown that I have personally encountered, along with the encounter visited in the chapter titled "The Thing in the Ditch."]

Swanson Lane is a road in west Knox County that is really just a long driveway onto private property (so a caveat is in order—don't go exploring without permission, please). I was friends with a lad in elementary school whose family lived in a house at the end of the road, which reached its terminus about a half a mile or more up at the top of a hill.

The lad in question was my best friend through second grade and onward in elementary school, and we took turns visiting each other's houses. One summer day when I was at my friend's house, we had ventured down the driveway, perhaps halfway, and were poking around in the remains of a shale pit dug into the side of a hill, looking for fossils.

Above us on the hillside sat perched an old farm shed of some sort. Prior to my friend's family purchasing the land, the whole area had been part of a massive farm comprising several hundred acres. Almost in unison, we looked up and spotted what I can only term as a creature. It stood on two legs, apparently, as it was looking at us from one of the windows of the broken-down, weed-covered shack. It had a head like a horse, but was jet black—the white eyes and somewhat human-looking teeth (which it was baring in what appeared to be a grin of rictus or hunger) stood out by comparison. It's possible that some sort of hoodlike apparatus was covering the head, because when comparing notes and illustrations later, we both remember it having X-like stripes between the eyes and in the forehead area, not unlike the Bay Area's "Zodiac" killer of a few years prior to this incident. (At the time, neither one of us was familiar with the Zodiac case—I'm only able to draw the similarities now after having studied the Zodiac in the 1990s. I'm sure the similarities are only coincidental.)

The horrible beast never offered to give chase, but it did make a noise, somewhere between a huffing and growling sound, which was what made us look in the direction where it stood initially. The bulging white eyes with dark pupils and those fang-like teeth were the stuff nightmares are made of. We both found our legs about the same time and ran, screaming at the top of our lungs, up the remaining quarter mile or so of the driveway to my friend's house.

When we arrived, breathless and crying, we were met by his parents in the front yard. It's very quiet way back there in the woods, and they had heard us coming up the driveway, such was the racket we were making with our screams and cries. There was a bit of skepticism on their part at first. It was obvious that something had frightened us, but they assured us there had to be some rational explanation for what we'd encountered. My friend's father went inside and retrieved a shotgun and went down the hill to check it out.

We waited nervously in the shade of an apple tree in the front yard, trying to calm ourselves with cherry Kool-Aid. We expected to hear shots and shouting, but it remained quiet. After what seemed like an eternity, my friend's father returned, shotgun slung over his shoulder. He seemed kind of off, like he'd seen something that had frightened him. He claimed to have not seen the beast, but admonished us both sternly for playing in the area and made us promise we wouldn't go near the shale pit or the shack up on top of it, for any reason. No worries there, as we fully intended to steer a wide berth around same. We both swore to never mess around down there, a promise we have kept to this day.

A few days later, my friend's father dragged the shack down into the shale pit with his tractor and set fire to it.

What had he seen that made him act this way? Although my friend and I discussed the myriad of possibilities for years afterwards, his father steadfastly refused to discuss any of it further. We even sat down independently of one another and drew a representation of what we saw—surprisingly (or maybe not so), the drawings were eerily similar.

As far as I know, the shale pit is most likely still there today. I moved away from the area more than a dozen years ago, but it had been at least twenty years prior to that since I had set foot on Swanson Road. The last time I was there, it wasn't a county road at all, but a really long gravel driveway. Again, this area is private property and I wouldn't recommend visiting without the express consent of the current owner. Even then, even if I had permission, I'm not sure I would want to revisit the area —I can still see the distorted countenance of the frightening beast in my mind's eye. Some things are better left alone and better left unknown.

CHAPTER SIX

OUIJA—WITH MOM AND BEYOND

[Have you ever played with a Ouija board, or any other type of "talking board," or "mystifying oracle"? Although I haven't had what I would consider a lot of experience with the board, I have used them and have been around where they were used constantly and to some great degree of accuracy. Some people love them, some people are afraid of them, and others laugh at what they consider the user's naivety and gullibility. Regardless of your opinion, I'll bet you have one regarding the Ouija.]

I was drawn to this type of thing as a small child, and I can remember my mother taking me to Woolworth's in the old downtown Oak Ridge shopping center. It must have been in the summer, as we took the board home and she showed me how to use it. My mother was no stranger to communicating with the other side—as a young girl, her family took part in the Spiritualism movement from around the turn of the last century. She often took part in seances, table-tapping sessions and Ouija sessions.

Those first sessions, I was amazed to feel the planchette moving beneath our fingertips. I at first thought my mother must be touching it, but I also recall that sometimes it would spell foreign words that she would have to look up the meaning of later on. Some of my first questions reflected my tender age (I was all of five): When would the first snowfall happen this year? How much snow would we get? What was I going to get for my birthday? For Christmas? I delighted in hearing the talking board spelling out many words that I didn't know, despite being precocious (I knew how to read at a third-grade level and had an extensive vocabulary, although I was only a kindergarten student).

My mother also explained the cautionary side of playing with the board. There were certain questions you must never ask ("When and how will I die?" and "When will the end of the world take place?" being two that I distinctly remember being sternly forbidden). She also stated that I must never play with the board alone, nor should I invite anything contacted via the board to join us on this plane of existence. These type of warnings and thoughts made me more than a little apprehensive, and while I would often think about the consequences just to scare myself, I obeyed and never took the board lightly or asked any of the questions I had been instructed not to ask.

I can remember another occasion when there was a particular phonograph record that I wanted desperately, but my parents had been unable to locate it locally. I asked my mother to help me consult the Ouija, and sure enough, it gave us the name of a somewhat obscure record shop in downtown Knoxville. A quick phone call (Oak Ridge to Knoxville was a long-distance call back then) when the shop opened later in the day confirmed that they did, indeed, have the record I wanted. My mother had them set it aside for us, and we went and purchased it after having lunch at Kress in Knoxville.

I was beginning to see the Ouija as a very useful tool, even at such a young age. This was when my mother let me know that too much Ouija could be a "bad thing," and relying on it for everyday decision-making would surely lead to a dire situation. So she put the Ouija board in the top of her closet, and it once again became a treat or something to use under special circumstances where "help from beyond the veil" was deemed necessary. Looking back, I'm very thankful that she taught me to use the talking board in moderation—as an adult, I have met those who have had their mind and their very life consumed by the Ouija, usually having been drawn to the dark side—which is easier than one might think. It starts out innocently enough, like me as a child, fascinated with the oracle and asking it a million inane questions, growing bolder and bolder each day. When it gets to the point of not being able to make any decision without the Ouija (or the tarot cards, or the zodiac or the star chart or runes or the I Ching or any number of systems of divinity) one risks becoming a slave to the practice.

By setting limits, I used the Ouija and other tools responsibly. Nowadays, I stay away from Ouija boards in general, but I do not fear them—like anything of an occult nature, I feel it only has the power over you that you give to it. While I would never tell anyone not to use a talking board (or recommend the use of one either), to each his or her own—use your due diligence and caution —otherwise I might end of writing about you in one of my future volumes!

CHAPTER SEVEN

THE METHODIST CEMETERY

[Just down the road from where I attended elementary school, on the other side of the Solway Church of God (yes, there are a lot of churches in the area), is what is referred to by residents of the community as the "Old Methodist Church," and accompanying cemetery. The cemetery is the final resting place for many of Solway's "old-timers" and family members. Given the fact that any cemetery can have a creepy vibe, especially at night, this cemetery is that times ten!]

The old Methodist Cemetery in the Solway community of west Knoxville, Tennessee, doesn't look like your typical haunted cemetery. For sheer size, age and beautifully carved old stones and monuments—truly a lost art —that local distinction would fall to Old Grey cemetery just off Broadway in downtown Knoxville.

The Methodist Cemetery, on the other hand, is just a good-sized country cemetery, with its bucolic setting, at the edge of a deep wood and just below a white, picturesque church that makes the cemetery seem so innocuous. On some of the nighttime excursions I've had to the location, I feel that the location is every bit as active as the fabled and infamous Beaver Ridge Cemetery on Copper Ridge Road discussed in another chapter. In fact, the Methodist Cemetery is located just across the roadway from another part of Beaver Creek. Perhaps it's something about the creek that helps create haunted cemeteries?

Once while on a date (yes, I have gone to a cemetery on a date—on more than one occasion), my date and I were standing in the middle of the tombstones when my lady-friend suddenly felt a bit too spooked and wanted a hug. As I obliged, she let out a little squeal and asked, "Did you see that?" Of course, I had been unable to see "that," whatever it was, because she was peering over my shoulder and I, hers. I pressed her for more information.

"It was a kid," she whispered excitedly. "He was peeking at us from behind that stone over there." She pointed to a massive headstone a few yards away. "What do you think a kid is doing in here this late at night?" she asked, perplexed. It was, after all, well after midnight.

I smiled in the darkness and began leading her back to the car. She was obviously sensitive enough to have spotted one of the familiar apparitions that some people see in the cemetery, but I was sure she would freak out when told that the little boy she had seen was not only not really there, but had been witnessed by people as much as four decades earlier. As predicted, when we got back to the warmth and safety of my automobile, she broke down into tears when I told her the legend of the boy. The date was over immediately, and she insisted on being taken home, where it took some cajoling on my part so that I could even leave for the night. It's been my experience that some people just aren't ready for an encounter with the unknown, no matter how badly they crave or desire one. It's nothing personal or demeaning, just some people handle things differently.

Much like the aforementioned Beaver Creek Cemetery, the wind and weather has been known to do strange things at the Methodist Cemetery. While you are as far away from the parking area as possible, it's not unusual for a strong wind to suddenly whip in, seemingly out of nowhere. Also the same with storm clouds, lightning, and pouring rain that will soak you to your skin. Once, I was pelted with marble-sized hail while exploring on a daylight trip into the cemetery. I ran to my car and left, only to have the weather return to clear skies by the time I had driven the mile or two back down to Oak Ridge Highway. When this happens, I simply take it that this isn't the proper time for a visit—for whatever reason—and plan on returning another day or night.

There is also a phenomenon here at the Methodist site that I have experienced in other cemeteries with this level of activity—there are certain stones that don't want to be photographed, at least not clearly or simply not at that time. The photo may blur slightly, or some other lens flare or odd type of photographic anomaly will occur. One example that readily springs to mind, there is the grave of a young girl whose headstone once held her favorite doll encased in glass on the back of the stone.

The glass and the doll have long since vanished, but the indention where the doll once stood can clearly be observed on the back of the stone. However, when trying to take a picture of said stone, I have experienced camera errors from blackened film back in the 35mm days to frozen shutters and battery and memory card malfunctions with modern, digital equipment. Sometimes, however, the stone can be photographed perfectly, with no problems whatsoever. Your guess is as good as mine as to the forces at work here...

The area itself seems a little off, and the nearness to Beaver Creek that I mentioned has a legend attached as well. Many years ago, when Solway was a busy stop on the L&N train line, two robbers on horseback got away with some money from the depot. They hid in a shallow cave along Beaver Creek, just down the hill from the cemetery, only to be found and subsequently killed by the law when they decided to shoot their way out rather than be hanged for their crime. It's said that if you stand in that area of the creek on a dark night, you can hear the sounds of hooves as two riders gallop past—on phantom steeds that can only be heard and not seen.

Although I personally have never had the privilege of fully spotting the apparition, it's rumored that a figure of a woman in a white dress can be seen flitting amongst the stones at night. The closest sighting I ever had for the White Lady was one night when I was tearing down Guinn Road by the cemetery headed for another location. I thought I saw a white figure, but in my haste I was already past before I could get a good look and confirmation. I turned around at Solway School Road and went back, but wasn't able to catch sight of anything further. On my return trip back, I actually stopped at the cemetery and sat in my car in the parking area, but had no luck that night—or any other. If you do visit and see the White Lady, by all means please drop me an email and let me know... The same holds true for *any* experience you might have here—as always, my email address and other contact information can be found at the end of this volume.

The Methodist Cemetery is open to the public and can be easily found on Google Maps of the area. As with any location, please use caution, common sense and—above all—the utmost respect for the deceased and their families when visiting. Also take note that the area behind the cemetery is posted positively NO TRESPASSING, and if you cross the fence, be prepared to suffer the consequences (or at least explain your actions to Knox County sheriff's deputies). There's nothing to see beyond the back fence anyway. Also, the area of the creek where the hoofbeats can be heard is, as far as I can gather at the current time, also private property. I have no knowledge of the current owner, but I'm sure the person one needs to secure permission from to visit could be found with relative ease if you're in the area. Asking at the KenJo market at the corner of Guinn Road and Oak Ridge Highway (right next to Dogwood Road) might be best.

CHAPTER EIGHT

HAUNTED HOUSE IN LAS VEGAS

[I lived on the west side of Las Vegas, just off West Sahara Blvd, in a house built in the 1930s. Now I'm no stranger to haunted houses—you'll find other stories in the book of places I've lived or visited that were haunted—but this one is the mother of them all, as far as hauntings go.]

During my tenure in Las Vegas, I worked for a while as a professional photographer. One of my models whom I worked with quite often on fashion, print and editorial products had asked me to visit her home for some specific shots she had in mind in her own surroundings. She lived in a wonderful stone and clapboard cottage, built in 1932. She had been to my studio several times, and we both enjoyed working with and trusted each other—I normally wouldn't travel alone to a model's home nor have a model alone in my studio, as it doesn't necessarily reflect the best business practices nor the safest environment for a model or photographer—I know both models who have been accosted by a Guy With Camera (photographer and model term for someone who's not really professional, but just looking to meet girls), as well as photographers who have been wrongly accused by Girl With Snapshots (another photographer and model term for someone who's not a professional model, but perhaps looking to blackmail or otherwise rip off true professionals, including photographers, other models, hairstylists, makeup artists, etc.).

So off I went, and we had an enjoyable evening photoshoot and captured all the poses she had in mind for her portfolio. Before I left, she gave me a tour of the house, and I was impressed at just how unusual the older "showplace" was. We both felt that the coolest (and creepiest) feature of the house was a completely hidden room behind a downstairs bookcase built into the wall.

My friend remarked how she loved the home, even though it was way too large for her needs. She had originally purchased the home while engaged, but she eventually caught on to her boyfriend's philandering ways and not only called the wedding off, but sent him and his things packing, leaving her all alone in five thousand square feet of "Old Vegas" opulence.

The walkout basement had five large rooms, plus the hidden rooms. The rooms on the back side of the house opened onto a patio with a koi pond with a waterfall and a parklike multilevel terrace and landscaped area. Inside, even though it was subterranean on one end, there was plenty of light and high ceilings. I casually mentioned she ought to consider renting the basement out to a photographer, as it would make a perfect studio space. She immediately asked me if I'd be interested, and I replied that I would, but I doubted I'd be able to afford the rent...

"You can have the entire basement, plus full use of the gourmet kitchen and upstairs common areas, for six hundred dollars a month," she replied. I darn near dislocated my arm whipping out my checkbook as fast as I could, writing her a check on the spot for first and last months' rent. Pleased with my good fortune, I went immediately to the current studio space I was renting and began packing the lights, backdrops, flash umbrellas and all the other pro photo equipment I had acquired during the last several years. My current landlord was a nervous church member and wasn't entirely keen on my having photoshoots on her property, although she had told me differently to lure me in. This was the same woman who became upset because I had used a bright red backdrop in my studio for a series of shoots, because (in her words) "red is the devil's color!" My new landlord had already said anything goes at her house, as long as it was legal. I was thankful to have such a freely creative, huge space for only a hundred bucks more than I'd been paying the other "Devil's Color" lady.

Within a few days, I had everything moved into the giant basement and set up my studio to my liking. Going from two small rooms to five huge rooms certainly spurred my imagination, and I started booking photo shoots right away, with the first one scheduled to happen in approximately three days.

On the day of the shoot, one of my regular models

was the first to arrive, so we decided to do some test shots before the hair stylist and makeup artist I'd hired for the session arrived. This was common procedure, sometimes known as "blocking out the shots," so I would know in advance where key lights, fills and bounces would need to go for optimal lighting of the subject. After about one hundred shots or so, we went upstairs to view the digital photos on a huge fifty-two-inch monitor I had set up in the living room—my new roommate didn't own a television, so she thought it was awesome to have such a large flat-screen in the beautiful appointed seating area.

As we scanned through the photos, making notes—the model on her poses, mine on lighting and composition—I noticed every so often the model would turn suddenly from the monitor and look directly at me. At first, I assumed she was just taking a very active and animated interest in the photographs, but as time went on, she seemed to start becoming quite agitated. Finally, unable to stand this odd display any longer, I asked her what was up.

"What's up with you?" she huffed back, giving me a pronounced pout. She wasn't really angry at me but clearly annoyed.

"What do you mean?" I asked, truly puzzled.

"It's just that I find it hard to concentrate on critiquing my poses with you saying rude things in my ear..."

I was flabbergasted. In retrospect, I'm glad this model knew me well and that we had shot together many, many times—especially after she told me some of the things she thought I'd said—mainly unflattering things about her body and poses.

Again, I was stunned. I would never treat a model that way! In fact, I had such a sterling reputation in Las Vegas that many beginning models came to me for their initial portfolio shoot—the models in a particular geographic area tend to gossip with one another—a lot——and photographers' names (both good and bad) make the rounds lightning quick. I was known for my patience and positive reinforcement and had never been rude or sarcastic to any of my clients. I assured her she must have heard something or someone else, as I had been quietly taking notes during the slideshow and hadn't uttered a single audible word to my knowledge. I paused the laptop connected to the giant flatscreen and went in the kitchen to make us both a glass of iced tea.

I'd only been in the kitchen for a few minutes when my model came skittering in, slid on the slick kitchen floor in her high heels, and knocked over a barstool at the breakfast counter. She was wild-eyed and obviously scared.

"Brooke? What's the matter?" I asked, concerned.

"I heard it," she said, her voice breaking. "I heard a voice in the living room! It whispered in my ear and told me I wasn't very pretty!"

She refused to leave the kitchen until I did, and she wasn't keen on going back into the living room at all. I decided we could go ahead and unhook everything and carry the drinks and laptop back downstairs to the studio. The other models and assistants for hair and makeup should be arriving soon. She breathed a sigh of relief and helped me get the gear and drinks downstairs, where we continued perusing the photos until the doorbell rang.

I went upstairs with Brooke right on my heels. Turns out my hair guy, Jeff, and Trina, the makeup artist, knew one another and had ridden in together. They brought the tools of their respective trades in and set up shop in the giant bathroom just off the hallway. Since Brooke had arrived first, she went into the chair first, and I continued fine-tuning the lights in the basement until the other models, three more in all, arrived. I ushered them into the living room and brought in a tray of bottled water and unsweetened drinks.

A few minutes (maybe fifteen minutes) later, I was back in the kitchen when two of the models, sisters named Samantha and Lisa, approached me conspiratorially. They were concerned that the other model, Jill, was up to something.

"Oh?" I asked the pair in hushed tones. "What did she do?"

"She's acting all weird," Samantha said as Lisa nodded in agreement. "She keeps looking at us all weird. And saying stuff."

"What kind of stuff?" I asked, suddenly realizing I already knew the answer.

"Crazy talk," Lisa chimed in, now Samantha nodding in agreement. "She's making snide remarks about the way we look and about our modeling experience. And she's doing it in this oddball voice. It's creeping us out!"

I promised I'd get to the bottom of it and sent the sisters downstairs to pick out some props and to arrange their wardrobe trunks. I walked into the living room with a fresh pitcher of lemon iced tea and offered some to Jill, who was sitting on the couch with a look of consternation on her face.

She waved away the iced tea, and I saw a single tear form in the corner of her eye.

"Jill, what's the matter?"

"It's *those* two," she snapped, pointing a thumb toward the stairs that led to the basement area. "I can't work around them if they continue to be so... so... unprofessional!"

I handed her a tissue and related the stories I'd been told by Brooke as well as Samantha and Lisa. Jill's eyes grew wide. She crossed herself and said she needed to leave. I begged her to stay, but her beliefs and superstitions wouldn't permit it. (In fact, Jill never came to my studio again—I shot with her on location afterwards, but she steadfastly refused to set foot in my "haunted" house.)

Brooke was just finishing her turn in the chair, so I brought the sisters up from the studio, and we all went out onto the terrace for a group meeting. At this point, I patched everyone's stories together and was able to get a better idea of the big picture. The rest of the girls agreed to stay, with Samantha and Lisa showing a very keen interest now that they thought it was a ghost rather than Jill trash-talking their modeling game.

The rest of the evening and night continued without incident, although we thought we heard footsteps on the hardwood-floored dining room upstairs. We broke around midnight, and Jeff and Trina left immediately.

Brooke, Samantha and Lisa stayed behind, asking if they could speak to me about an idea they had. I said, "Sure, why not?" and we went out on the rooftop terrace to take in the cool night air of the desert.

"We'd like to hold a seance," Brooke said, speaking for the group. "What do you think of that?"

I allowed that it was agreeable, and it might even be fun. I was truly interested to see what spirits might be at the house, having had a lifelong interest in anything strange or creepy. We finished our drinks and the girls all departed into the night. We had decided on the following Saturday night for the seance.

After what seemed like an eternity of anticipation, Saturday finally arrived. I had cancelled my original photoshoot and booked one with Brooke, Samantha and Lisa. This way, I could kill two birds with one stone, so to speak—I could get the fashion product shoots a client had asked for and still be able to have the seance. Working for yourself sometimes means having to be financially creative. Since the client's product was footwear, I wouldn't even need hair and makeup assistance on this particular shoot. Things were going smoothly.

We finished the shoot in record time, and the girls all changed into comfortable clothes for the seance. Samantha and Lisa were heavily into the occult, so they brought a giant Rubbermaid storage bin full of things they thought we would need, including candles, sea salt, sage and a Ouija board. I was kind of amazed to see them covering all the mirrors in the house with black cloth. They claimed it was standard operating practice for hauntings, to either keep evil spirits from escaping through the mirrors or coming into the house out of the mirror. I found the duality of the concept interesting.

Brooke wasn't as into the occult as the sisters, but she was dating a guy who, in her own words, was part of a "satanic metal band," so she knew enough about the paranormal to be fascinated yet keep anything truly evil at a respectful distance.

It was decided by all involved that the seance should begin in the secret room behind the bookshelf in the basement and then continue upstairs and elsewhere, depending on the initial outcome. My roommate was away visiting family in Northern California for the weekend, so we would be undisturbed in that regard. I went through the house unplugging clocks (another request from the sisters), shutting off any unnecessary electronics, and then finally shutting off all the lights, inside and out, throwing the house and surrounds into total darkness. Incredibly, it was like flipping a switch in more ways than one—as the lights went out, there was a noticeable, very palpable charge in the air. Brooke noticed it as well and gripped my hand tightly in the darkness as the sisters lit long black taper candles, and we followed them single file into the basement.

I opened the heavy oak bookcase on its heavy hinges at the bottom of the stairs, and we all slipped inside the roughly twenty-five-by-twenty-five-foot room. When the bookcase snapped closed, it was as if all the air was sucked out of the hidden anteroom. The light from the candles even seemed dimmer in this hidden chamber, and the unlit corners of the room seemed blacker than black. The rest of us watched as Samantha drew a circle of protection around us on the bare concrete floor using the sea salt. She admonished us that no matter what, we all had to remain within the circle until such a time as she had "broken" it. We all sat within the confines of the circle, which went right up to the very walls of the square room, only leaving the corners unprotected. All but one of the tapers was extinguished, and with light wisps of smoke and the smell of burning wax in the air, Samantha led the group in a brief prayer, and then the seance officially began.

Personally, I was relieved to see that the Ouija board had not been brought into the confined space with us, as I still have mixed feelings about the safety and sanity of using the "mystifying oracle" as either a tool of divination or as a means of contacting the great beyond. The reprieve was short-lived though, as I would find out later when we went upstairs into the living room.

Samantha and Lisa had done this sort of thing many times, apparently. Brooke and I watched silently as the sisters called out to the spirits of the universe as well as any spirits in or near the house. We both nearly jumped out of our skin when we heard a noise upstairs in the otherwise empty house. Brooke had my hand in a death grip, and I looked over to see her eyes tightly closed. Samantha and Lisa continued their callings, with Samantha apparently slipping into a mild trance as she welcomed the spirits of the house to our little gathering.

I was just reconsidering how this might have not been such a good idea (in fact, I was thinking at that very moment that this may well be a Very Bad Idea), when suddenly the candle snuffed out. If I thought the air was gone out of the room, it was that times ten now. Brooke stifled a scream as the icy, inky blackness surrounded us. Samantha took the opportunity to remind us not to leave the protection of the salt circle until she gave the clearance to do so. No worry on that —I was glued to the spot and Brooke was glued to me— we weren't going anywhere right now, at least not without a fight. Brooke had always claimed she considered me a father figure, so I suppose that explains why she felt protected. We shivered in the darkness as Samantha and Lisa both proclaimed aloud—the spirits had arrived.

Thankfully, Samantha announced that we needed to move to another part of the house. She had relit the tapers and had performed some sort of banishing to anything outside the circle, and then carefully scraped open a "door" in the salt circle through which we could all safely depart. We gathered outside the hidden room (which I'll admit, I was in fear that the bookcase simply wouldn't open and we'd all be trapped with the ghosts. I'm glad that wasn't the case), and Samantha and Lisa began discussing where we should go next while standing on the wooden stairs. The group ventured to the first landing and almost went out the French doors to one of the many outdoor terraces on the property. Instead, Samantha felt that her "spirit guide" was pointing her toward farther upstairs in the living room, so we followed suit. We marched single file into the living room, which looked even eerier than usual when lit only by candlelight. I followed Samantha's lead, and we all formed a circle around a low wooden table in the middle of the room.

Again, she used the sea salt to cast a circle of protection around us (in case you're wondering, the salt did vacuum out of the vintage 1970s shag carpet with no difficulty the next day), and this time Lisa retrieved the Ouija board from their plastic bin, which contained a veritable Pandora's box of occultic and Spiritualism goodies. Now it was my turn to have a death grip on Brooke's hand. She didn't seem to mind the Ouija board, although I found small comfort in that. Thankfully, Samantha and Lisa declared that they would be the mediums to use the board, and Brooke and I would remain as observers. Now that did give me a bit of comfort and relief.

Once again, all the candles save for one were extinguished, and the sisters—staying well within the confines of the circle of protection—sat facing each other, knees touching, with the Ouija board between them. Brooke and I watched in silence as they began the task. Both with eyes closed, heads tilted back, the planchette between them moving slowly, describing a sideways figure eight —an infinity symbol.

After a few minutes, an entity had made itself known via the Ouija board. It informed us his name was Pieter and he had immigrated to the United States from Germany just after the first World War. Further, he had lived in the house in Las Vegas in the 1950s, and claimed to have died in a traffic accident on Boulder Highway sometime in the late 1960s. Other than those very specific facts, Pieter didn't have a lot to say and was happy to move on off the Ouija board and allow others to come in, as he also claimed there were many, many spirits waiting to have a word with the sisters and their "magical conduit," as he called the device.

Another spirit claimed to have been a mob boss who had once stayed in the house briefly as a "safe house," but then he had been double-crossed and murdered execution style in the basement by the very men he trusted. He refused to identify himself and also stated that he was very angry and was bent on revenge.

As a side note, the house was built in 1931. This was prior to anything being built on now-famous Las Vegas Strip, where real-life gangster opened the Flamingo in December of 1946. So at the time my house was built, it would have been in practically the middle of nowhere— the only casinos and hotels in existence in 1932 would have been in the downtown area of Las Vegas, on and around Fremont Street, which was a few miles from where I lived off West Sahara and Arville Street. I was told, indeed, by the neighbors at the end of the street who had been there since 1950, that the house had been a mafia safe house at one time. They also added that for a period of time, from the mid-1950s until possibly as late as the early 1970s, the house had been home to some sort of "strange religious cult" (their words) who held services in the cavernous basement. The mafia bits and the weird cultists explain a lot and will explain even more later on...

Now, I had never mentioned any of the facts passed to me from the people who lived at the end of the street. So, unless they were clever secret investigators, the sisters had no way of knowing any of the history of the house. In fact, they were from Colorado, where they had been born, and had only been in Las Vegas for a few months. Brooke didn't know any of the house's history, nor did any of my friends. Even my roommate, who owned the property, knew nothing of its past—I'd had a chance encounter with the elderly neighbor from down the street one day when I was out gathering the mail, and he stated he often wondered who could live in "such a house" and asked if we had any idea of the dark history contained within its walls.

Sure enough, one of the later spirits the sisters contacted via the Ouija board claimed to have been summoned to the house "decades ago, by a high priest." At this point, I'd heard all that I wanted to hear, as I still had to stay in the house—and alone over the weekend at that! Samantha agreed, broke the circle, and everyone drifted off into the night. I did promise that I would keep all my seance guests informed of any paranormal or otherwise strange or unexplained activity in the house, and would report back to them on a future photoshoot. Although spooked, I plied myself with an excellent Shiraz and quickly enough fell asleep alone in the dark, dark house.

The next evening, I didn't have anything scheduled other than looking through some photos I was editing in Photoshop. Around 9 p.m., my eyes needed a rest and I was just preparing a bath when the front doorbell rang. I answered it immediately, only to find no one there. Neighborhood kids, I surmised, having done similar pranks as a child. I closed the door and walked into the bathroom and prepared to draw a bath in the sunken tub.

The doorbell rang again. Once again, no one was there. Darn kids.

After just starting to relax in the hot bath I'd drawn in the enormous garden tub, I heard a strange noise coming from somewhere in the house. It sounded as if someone were dragging a full metal garbage can down either the hallway or in the dining room—the only rooms in the house with wooden floors. This continued for a few minutes, and I finally decided my roommate had returned early from visiting her family in Northern California. The noises eventually subsided, and I relaxed for the better part of an hour before I made myself get out and towel off, lest I totally prune myself. Slipping on an oversized terry cloth robe I'd brought home from Hong Kong, I walked out into the cool dark house. I called out to my roommate a few times, but never received a response. I walked back to her room, which was dark with the door open. No one was home. I even went and peeked out the side windows in the parking area. The double security gate was firmly closed, and only my automobile was parked in the carport. Again, I simply thought it was odd but not too strange. I shrugged it off and went inside to watch a movie while waiting until it was time to turn in for the night.

Sometime during the night, I woke up—wide awake—I had fallen asleep on the sectional suede sofa in the living room, something I rarely (if ever) did. The movie was over and the plasma TV, sensing there was no longer a signal, had shut itself off. Then I heard the noise again—the heavy trash can dragging noise—and had the startling revelation that was what had awakened me from my deep slumber on the couch. The house was dark and, other than the weird scraping noise, totally silent. I rolled off the sofa onto the shag carpet and slowly began making my way toward the hall. As I crept by the fireplace, I thought to snag the poker, just in case. Granted, it wasn't much of a weapon, but better than nothing, I surmised.

I could see a bit of moonlight spilling across the landing where the stairs from the basement terminated, but could only see the near end of the hallway. The other end, where the noises—which had now conveniently stopped—sounded like they had been coming from, was cast in total pitch-black darkness. I stealthily rose on one knee and groped blindly for the light switch, poker at the ready in what I hoped was an intimidating position. I switched the light on and leapt to my feet, brandishing the poker wildly—to a completely empty hallway. I blinked my eyes a few times and strained to listen. Nothing, the only noise was the refrigerator and the near-silent hum of the house's two rooftop air-conditioning units. A quick check of the other rooms, even downstairs, turned up no intruders—at least not physical ones. The security system that covered all the windows and doors was still armed, and there was no indication that anyone had been in the house through any other means. I shut everything back off and tried to go back to sleep in my bedroom. Sleep didn't come again until I saw the sun beginning to peek over the western horizon.

When my roommate returned from northern California, she brought along a new addition to the household—a little dog, half Corgi, half German shepherd (yes, he looked as odd as he sounds, but he was a sweet little fellow), named Captain Stubbs. Imagine a miniature German shepherd with tiny, short little legs and you get the idea.

Right away, Captain Stubbs and I became best friends. I think he may have been part "chow" hound (haha!) because he sure did love to eat. I enjoyed cooking in the gourmet kitchen, which my roommate loved because she didn't have any idea how to cook—I often made dinner for the three of us, Captain Stubbs included.

There was also something else I noticed right away—Captain Stubbs' reluctance to visit certain parts of the house. The areas he shied away from were the room downstairs that had supposedly been a cult sanctuary, the hidden room behind the bookcase, and the upstairs hallway (where I had heard the mysterious sounds of the "full metal trash can" being dragged on the hardwood). I chalked it up to being in an unfamiliar area, but I soon came to realize that Captain Stubbs wouldn't go into those areas for any reason, even for his favorite treat from my cooking—the "Chef's Surprise" with fried eggs.

One day, I was home alone and heard a bone-chilling howl that made the hair stand up on my arms and neck. It sounded as if someone was being murdered. A quick jog through the house and I found the source of the din —Captain Stubbs had bravely tried to traverse the dark hallway to get into the kitchen where his food and water were placed. Under normal circumstances, he would trot out the doggy door in my roommate's suite, around the house, up the terrace, and then back in through another doggie door on the first landing on the basement stairs. For whatever reason, he had tried a different route on this day, and what I witnessed was hard to believe.

Captain Stubbs was on the floor on his belly, howling like mad. It was as if some unseen force was holding him down, firmly enough that, despite trying with all his might, he couldn't crawl away or back up or even stand on his stubby little legs. Stymied, and sure that the dog was injured in some way, I headed down the hallway to see what I could do to help him out, envisioning an emergency trip to the vet's office.

However, just as I got almost to where he was, I felt some sort of cold spot pass through me. Yes, that's what I said—it passed through me, instead of me passing through it. I stopped in my tracks, my entire body suddenly covered in goose bumps. Instantly, Captain Stubbs' paralysis broke. He immediately stopped the unearthly howling and literally jumped up and ran into my roommate's room, where he peered back at me from around the corner of the doorjamb. I went in the kitchen and got out some food and called for him. Sure enough, in a couple of minutes, he entered via the doggy door near the stairs to the basement and trotted through the living room and into the kitchen, eyes bright, tail wagging.

As Captain Stubbs devoured his din-din, I gave him a cursory inspection. Nothing appeared out of the ordinary. He had no lumps or limps or sprains or broken bones, and his appetite was surely one hundred percent intact. I sent a text message to my roommate and let her know about the incident. Later, after hearing me describe what had happened a couple of times, she packed Captain Stubbs in her Jeep and tore off to the vet's office, better safe than sorry. As it turned out, Captain Stubbs got a completely clean bill of health, and the vet was as mystified as we were regarding the poor little dog's reaction.

Going forward, my roommate also noticed Captain Stubbs' odd behavior and apparent inability to go certain places in the house. If the doggie door in my roommate's room was locked, the dog was content to stay in her bedroom and soil the carpet rather than venture down the hallway. When she mentioned it to the vet on another visit, the vet remarked how unusual this was, especially for such a crate-trained and well-housebroken canine.

During my time living in the house, my roommate tried to deny anything unusual was going on. She even tried to discount the weird behavior by Captain Stubbs as "some sort of dog mind thingy we just don't understand," as she put it. However, the incident that finally made her a believer—as much as she could believe, I suppose—happened one day while I was out at Red Rock Canyon for a photo shoot with a bevy of models for a local cosmetics startup.

My roommate was relaxing on the bed in her room, reading, when she heard what sounded like the downstairs door open, followed shortly by several voices. As the voices grew louder, she heard laughter and then low music. As the music swelled, the voices dropped to a murmur. She said the music sounded like organ music, the kind one might have heard at—yes—a church. She assumed I had finished early and had brought some of the models over to go through digital photographs, which is what I usually did.

Taking her time, she got up, put on a caftan and went into the kitchen and made herself a drink. The music continued, then stopped, and she heard voices again. She could tell it was for sure a male voice, assuming it was me, but couldn't quite make out what I was saying. Being a model herself as well, she decided to come down and join us. As she made her way down the stairs, about three steps from the bottom she recalls, suddenly everything became silent. Curiously, she continued down the stairs and into my darkened studio. Looking into the other rooms, she saw that they all were very dark and very empty. She even switched on the lights and looked into the storage areas—and the hidden room behind the staircase—but there simply wasn't anyone or anything to be found, let alone an after-shoot party with a dozen models.

Not fully understanding what had just happened, she even wandered outside, only to find hers was the only vehicle in the carport. She went back in, went to her room, grabbed her cell phone, and immediately called me. As luck would have it, I was just setting up my cameras and tripods in another area of the canyon when I received the call. I listened to her story and assured her I had been in Red Rock Canyon since 6 a.m., and would be there for a few more hours (this was around noon). She suddenly sounded on the verge of hysteria and asked if she could come out to the location. "Sure," I replied, I could always use an extra set of hands at a photo shoot. She arrived shortly, looking very shaken.

When we returned home in separate vehicles that evening, she couldn't stop talking about her experience. *Now you know how I've felt all my life*, I thought. I held my tongue though—who am I to judge? I let her fully explain and accepted what she had heard—something impossible, something that was inexplicable, something that bore no rational nor scientific explanation. Although I've never been one to say "I told you so," I felt somewhat vindicated. It is a nice thing, in a way, to see someone experience something that takes their belief system and completely turns it on its head. It certainly gives you something to ponder about and may cast things in a completely new light. Speaking of light, my roommate now refused to sleep without a night light. She also asked that I sleep on the couch—just for one night—in case she had a nightmare—or if the phantom organist and his party people returned. I obliged her—I had learned previously that the suede sectional sofa (for which she'd paid the princely sum of $3500) was very comfortable. The next morning, she allowed that she had slept fitfully, waking up every little bit, but that other than the usual noises of the house (that had caused her to jump at even the tiniest creak), everything was silent and peaceful.

It also gave her new insight into Captain Stubbs. A lot of experts claim that animals are more sensitive to the paranormal than people are, generally, so this made sense to her. Captain Stubby had encountered some phantom of his own—some malevolent spirit, bent on punishing the little doggie and preventing him from eating his delicious food. My roommate became very caught up in the paranormal, reading every book she could get her hands on concerning ghosts and hauntings. She also began frequenting Bell, Book and Candle, a famous occult bookshop in Las Vegas. She even brought home sage, incense and sea salt to help cleanse the house.

Another incident happened with the built-in shelves in my bedroom. I had a length of thick wooden dowel rod inserted between two holders where I hung up my dress pants, oxford shirts, and blazers. One particular night, after it had all fallen a couple of times (although the weight was not that much for the size of the wooden bar), I grabbed some tools and hardware from the garage and put a wood screw in each end of the dowel and through the U-shaped holders on each end of the rod.

"Now," I said aloud, "let's see you throw those on the floor!"

Satisfied with my handiwork, I turned out the light and hopped back into bed. My head had no more hit the pillow than I heard all my carefully hung clothing flop down onto the floor. I leaped from the bed, angry, and switched on the lights—and found the bar still screwed in place.

Every single piece of clothing, however, was still on the hangers and laid in a perfectly straight line on the floor, each piece overlapped by the one after it. It reminded me of toppled dominoes.

"You've GOT to be KIDDING!" I shouted aloud to the empty room. I considered taping the hangers to the rod, but it was getting late—after two in the morning by that time—and I really didn't want to throw down the gauntlet and issue any more challenges that night. Instead, I picked up the clothes in several different batches and hung them on a similar bar in the laundry room on the other side of the house. I left them there and never had any more problems—well, at least not with the clothes—after that incident.

Probably the most disturbing incident that happened where I was involved occurred just a few months before I left Las Vegas for Portland, Oregon.

I had a relatively new model over, maybe her third or fourth shoot in my studio. She was a recent transplant from Detroit and what I considered very tough—she had a lot of tattoos and talked of fighting her way out of nasty predicaments in the urban jungle that is modern-day Detroit. Regardless of all that, I had a client who needed just such a tough, tattooed and pierced look for a leather clothing shop. We were working our way through the product line for his website for items that she could wear, while I sought other models for the other bits.

On this night shoot, we were in the middle room of my studio against a faux brick wall I had paid to have installed. The studio lights were hot, the hair and makeup girls were having trouble keeping everything looking fresh, and I'm sure the model was roasting alive in the heavy leather products she was modeling for the cameras.

Suddenly, just as I snapped off a series of fifteen photos in "burst" mode (where the camera fires off the frames in sequence as fast as it can), I noticed something red on the model's right leg through the viewfinder.

As I called it to her attention, she spun around, and the makeup girl let out a stifled little shriek.

"Oh my God," she said, pointing at the back of the model's leg in the calf area, "you're bleeding!"

Sure enough, in the light it was easy to see that there were three fresh, fairly deep gouges on her calf, and the blood was headed toward her ankle. The slashes were in a row, equally spaced about half an inch apart and approximately three inches long. I grabbed a towel off the makeup tray and tossed it to her. She held it in place to staunch the bleeding.

I had the camera connected to a laptop on a stand, so I started looking through the last burst as my makeup and hair girls applied first aid. The shoot wasn't officially over as far as I was concerned—we could shoot around the wound without a lot of fanfare. I found the shots and the burst, and I'm sure my jaw dropped open. In one shot, her leg was fine—but in the next frame, less than a second later, the ugly scratches were clearly visible. They were so fresh, they hadn't even started bleeding much until the final frames of the burst.

I walked over to the brick wall by where she had been standing and inspected it very carefully. There was nothing—no wire, no shard of brick, no nail—there was nothing on the wall that could have made those scratches. Plus, when looking at the photos again, it was clear that she was *facing* the wall when the scratches appeared. One frame nothing; the next, bloody scratches.

By this point I was stymied, and it looked like my assistants had patched her up pretty good, including some triple antibiotic ointment for added safety. But instead of continuing as I had figured we would, the model was angry and livid. She cursed up a storm and started packing up her things. *Now* the shoot was officially over. I tried to apologize, to reason with her, but she wasn't having any of it. She continued to escalate until she was almost shrieking:

"You don't understand," she finally yelled in my face, "three marks! Three!"

I looked at her questioningly. I had no idea what she was talking about.

"There's something demonic here," she continued yelling. "Any time anyone gets three scratches, it's a mockery of the Holy Trinity!"

You could have heard a pin drop. Unbeknownst to me at the time, although I found out all about it later, what she was saying is correct in paranormal investigation circles. Apparently she had been involved with some paranormal groups in Detroit and knew that of which she spoke. Although we continued to correspond via email and text message, we never worked together again —and I can't say as I blame her. It was only a few weeks later I got the opportunity to move to Portland, and I jumped at the chance, although I personally was never injured by the house's resident demon.

After I moved, my roommate struggled on in the house, still mostly in outward denial about the events taking place, but inwardly, she remained very afraid of what might happen. Finally, after a worsening string of roommates who caused problems (and unsuccessful attempts to lure me back to Las Vegas from Portland), she found herself very much upside down in a huge mortgage for a house she no longer loved or even wanted, so she walked away. The house was eventually short sold, and I have no clue as to the experiences that may have been had by the current tenants, but I'll never forget my days (and nights) in the very active haunted house in Las Vegas.

CHAPTER NINE

HAUNTED BALLY'S CASINO, LAS VEGAS

[People have haunted houses, but a haunted job? Here's one of my encounters from Las Vegas concerning the experiences I had while working in a haunted casino—Bally's. The Bally's casino on the strip in Las Vegas has a long and tragic history. It was the original site of the MGM Grand, which was partially destroyed by fire in 1980, causing eighty-two people to lose their lives.]

For a couple of years in the mid-2000s, I managed the in-house photo lab at Bally's Hotel and Casino on the Las Vegas Strip. What a lot of people don't realize is that the current Bally's is really just a retrofit of the previously existing towers where people died, with the new section facing the Las Vegas Strip.

The company I worked for had the souvenir photo concession for all the major casinos in Las Vegas. If you've ever been to a show in Vegas or had a meal in one of the more upscale restaurants in the casinos, you've no doubt been approached by a "camera girl" (or boy, as the case may be) asking to take your photo to preserve the moment for posterity. After they get several shots, they scurry off to the photo lab (generally hidden in the bowels of the casino) to have the pictures printed. Then, upon their return, they have the photos all nicely packaged in simulated faux leatherette albums, and try their best to hustle you for as much as they can. As with practically everything in Vegas, it's meant to fleece the flock, and does so very well—the owners of the photography concession have been doing business in Las Vegas casinos since the 1960s and own such multimillionaire fluff as McMansions and Maybach automobiles (no lie) to show for their efforts.

At Bally's, the photo lab was located on the second floor, just above the showroom where "Jubilee!" (one of Vegas' remaining showgirl review holdovers) and other shows are presented. If you've ever seen any of the footage of the old Dean Martin "Celebrity Roasts" from the 1970s, you've seen the showroom—they are one and the same—these roasts were held at the old MGM, pre-fire, of course.

The area upstairs above the theater is known as the "Celebrity Hallway" and is where the Green Room and celebrity dressing rooms were located for the Dean Martin shows (and anything else performed and/or broadcast from the old MGM). Down at one end of the hallway, snugged back into a corner, is the photo lab. At one time, the camera girls used actual film cameras and would scurry back to the lab only to have to wait on the chemical process that developed the film and photos.

The advent of digital photography has changed the souvenir photography landscape—no longer is there any film to be developed, and even the labs that still use a "wet" printer (meaning it has tanks that hold liquid developer, bleach and water) can have your photos ready to go in a matter of minutes.

The lab at Bally's has smaller rooms where giant chemical tanks sit empty, silent reminders of the film photography legacy of days gone by—the place has a very old, almost abandoned feel to it, even though it is in use seven days a week, 365 days a year (as the casinos never close, so goes the souvenir photo concession). It was mainly in the smaller anterooms where the strangeness resided.

Other than the general feeling of something being off and not right just from walking into the photography lab, I began experiencing things from the very start. As the manager, I was the lab key holder and usually arrived an hour or so before the lab officially went into operation. I fired up the machinery and made sure all the Nikon cameras, Speedflash units and batteries were all good and ready to go.

On my first day alone at Bally's, I unlocked the door, turned on the lights, and walked right into what I can only describe as a "column" of ice-cold air. The column seemed to dissipate quickly, and I chalked it up to perhaps faulty air conditioning or having something to do with opening the lab doors after they had been sealed for fifteen hours or so. I shrugged it off and went about my business of getting the wet photo printer and cameras ready for the night's activities.

I walked into one of the back rooms to remove some Nikon batteries from their chargers and noticed a couple of things: One, the electrical access panel on the wall was open, revealing all the breakers for the lab. I closed the hinged access panel and snapped the latch, making sure it was secured firmly. Two, I noticed that another back room off the one I was in was open. It had a sliding wooden pocket door and had originally been the darkroom back in the days when the lab processed actual film. Darkroom was a most fitting sobriquet—the room looked to be pitch black just beyond the doorway. I peeked in, found it empty, and slid the pocket door closed, turning the latch.

After readying the cameras and accompanying flash units with fresh batteries, I set about firing up the wet printer. It had a series of self-tests and strips it processed to ensure that the chemical mix in the bleach and developer tanks was correct. After starting this process, I walked back into the room where the batteries had been charging in order to charge the used batteries I had just taken out of the cameras and flash units. Rounding the corner, two things immediately struck me—the electrical access panel was open again, ajar about two or three inches. Also, the darkroom door was not only open again as well, the one dim bulb that hung from the ceiling was also lit...

More perplexed than scared, I tried to brush it off. I knew I was the only person in the lab. I had unlocked the door myself and had locked it behind me—it would remain so until about a half hour before my photographers and other support personnel were due to arrive.

Plus, the lab, while cavernous in some regards, was actually a series of small rooms—there was no way anyone could have come in or have been already hidden inside without being seen. Dutifully, I closed and latched the panel again. I also slid the pocket door closed after turning out the sole light in the old darkroom.

A few minutes later, I once again walked in the back to retrieve some large rolls of Kodak photographic paper, which I would need to get through the number of prints that would be made that evening. And, once again, I was not really surprised to find the electrical access panel open (this time instead of just a crack, it was opened and flung back as far as possible), the pocket door was completely open, and the light was on again in the darkroom.

"Alright, fine," I said aloud to the empty lab. "If you want things that way, I'll leave them that way."

And I did. The electrical access panel remained open, the pocket door open, and the darkroom light on. This seemed to appease whatever I was dealing with, and I didn't have any more trouble. A lot of times at the end of the shift, I would shut the same doors and turn the darkroom light off only to find the doors open and the light on the next day when I opened the lab, although I had been the last to leave and no one had been in afterwards.

One day, while I was opening the lab and getting ready for the night's photo printing, one of my bosses, a large Serbian man named Gordan, dropped by the lab to bring some new larger memory cards for the cameras.

"I always hated when I had to work in this lab," he stated, having started as a lab manager and worked his way up into middle management. "It always felt like I was being watched, and there's a door that won't stay closed and a light that won't stay turned off." I nodded my head in agreement, even though he didn't mention the access panel. He stuck his head into the darkroom and then hurriedly left. I got the distinct feeling he'd had other, slightly more sinister experiences.

Another time, I was sitting in the lab waiting for the photographers to arrive. My "runners" that evening (runners helped the photographers package and sell their shots after the show broke) were two Hispanic cousins, still in their late teens. We were just sort of sitting and shooting the breeze when all of a sudden a very strange thing happened. A black, shapeless "mist" (for lack of a better description) came out of a wall of cabinets, crossed through the room we were in (about twenty-five feet) and then disappeared into the opposite wall.

I wasn't going to say anything, just to make sure my eyes weren't playing tricks on me—but it turns out I didn't have to—the cousins erupted with shock, surprise and quite a bit of profanity. They had seen the same thing that I had witnessed, and were both scared out of their wits. They took it as some sort of omen or warning and insisted that they had to leave immediately. I tried in vain to talk them into staying, but they signed out and left the premises. We got through the night with the help of another runner sent over from Caesar's Palace and myself. I didn't mention the black shape to anyone and observed no ill-effects from the manifestation.

There was also an entity in a nearby men's room that myself and a cameraman (who claimed to be a sensitive or psychic) dubbed "the Snorer." This was due to the fact that at certain times, both day and night (we opened the lab early on Saturdays for matinee shows in the Jubilee! Theater), we could hear what sounded like someone contentedly snoring away in the very last stall, enjoying a snooze on the job. The thing was, however, we both verified several times that the stall in question was empty, and my cameraman even claimed to have once heard the snoring while he was *inside* the very stall. I always avoided it, because the snoring and occasional stirring and shifting sounds already made me feel intrusive, just being in the same restroom, let alone the same stall. We gathered that perhaps the Snorer was an employee of the old MGM who was napping on the job and died of smoke inhalation...

All in all, Bally's was—shall we say—a very interesting place to work. I put in a couple of years as lab manager before being promoted out to the Rio Hotel and Casino, which is another story for another time—the Rio's VooDoo Steakhouse Lounge on the top of the casino had its own unexplained activity.

CHAPTER TEN

THE TELEPATHIC PHONE CALL

[The death of a family member is never an easy thing to deal with, but having the precognition of that death, even if only for a moment, can easily add to the devastation.]

I remember it was summer. I was a teenager, and lounging about doing nothing was satisfying due to the extreme heat and humidity that year. I was just barely in my teens, so not really old enough for a summer job or old enough to drive or do anything even remotely fun.

I had finished breakfast and had piled onto the couch in our family room to watch television. Apparently bored with whatever fare MTV or HBO had to offer pre-noon, I promptly drifted off back to sleep.

I was in the middle of a strange dream. It was one of those where you're awake enough to know that you're dreaming, but not fully awake to "wake up," as it were. In the dream, I was surrounded by a thick, inky blackness.

My first thought was "this is what it would be like to be inside a coffin."

I also noticed a low murmuring of voices in the background, both male and female. I couldn't hear what was being said, but I could tell by the tone of the voices that something somber and serious was being discussed. In addition to the sounds of polite conversation, I could hear the faint strains of instrumental music in the background, and there was something about flowers... and then it hit me—what I was experiencing was a crowd gathered... to pay their respects... at a funeral home. A sadness washed over me, as I had the grim realization that someone had died, someone close... The ringing of the telephone jolted me awake.

I groggily made my way into the bathroom to splash some cold water on my face, when I heard a piteous wail from the kitchen, where the phone was, and then the sound of deep, heaving sobbing. I raced out of the bathroom and into the kitchen and found my mother crying heavily. Momentarily, she quietly placed the telephone handset back into the cradle.

"Little Wayne is dead," she said between sobs. Little Wayne was my uncle's son. He was very young, only seven years old. It was later found that he had perished tragically in a house fire. His mother, who was divorced from my uncle, shared custody of Wayne and another child from a different marriage. She had fallen asleep while smoking in bed, and the mattress had smoldered for hours rather than bursting into full flame. All three had died of smoke inhalation. The mattress had eventually stopped smoking, and that was the reason the bodies had gone undiscovered for several days, according to the county coroner.

This scenario bothered me for years. I couldn't understand that, if I was going to have a precognitive dream, why couldn't I have it in time to help someone out? Granted, the boys and their mother had already been dead for days when I had the dream—but to have a dream like that—only to be awakened by the phone ringing to deliver the sad news of a death in the family, weighed on me heavily.

Years later, I had another experience with a precognitive dream that springs readily to mind. This time, instead of going back down for a nap after breakfast, I was actually going to bed at a normal time. That alone should have been a warning that something extraordinary was about to happen—I have been a notorious "night owl" since childhood, and as an adult rarely get to bed before two or three in the morning. As a writer, overcast, rainy "gray days" and the dead of night from midnight onward are my most creative times—there's just something about it that inspires me to crank up some '80s synthpop with a bit of new wave and write like mad, sometimes only stopping from sheer exhaustion or when I notice the first thin rays of light beginning to break over the eastern horizon.

So, here I was actually going to bed around eleven in the evening. I was unusually tired and ready to snooze. I don't think my head had more that hit the pillow when I found myself in the middle of a strange, vivid dream.

I was on a busy construction site, obviously somewhere in the South, based on the preponderance of "red clay mud" that seemed to be everywhere. The site was a den of activity, and people in jeans, plaid shirts, work boots and hard hats scurried to and fro, each with their own assignment or tasks to be accomplished. I glanced off to my left and noticed an impressive stack of concrete drainage pipes.

On closer inspection, I could see that although the huge pipes (each probably measuring three feet across) had been arranged in a pyramidal stack, they weren't in any way secured.

"That's dangerous," I said to myself in the dream. "Those pipes could collapse and…"

Before I could get the words out of my mouth in the dream, I watched in horror as the stack of pipes did, indeed, collapse just as a man was walking by. The pipes rolled over him and bounced off down the hill, coming to rest against a huge piece of yellow construction machinery. The man's mangled, twisted, crushed body was the most vivid and graphic thing I have ever seen in a dream. I had literally watched him popped like a grape, with huge quantities of blood and organs at both ends. I turned away and retched… and then I sprang wide awake. I sat up in bed, drenched in a cold sweat and shivering despite the heat. I must have cried out, as I had awakened my then girlfriend as well.

"Are you okay?" she asked, wiping sweat from my forehead. "You look like you've seen a ghost."

"Worse," I rasped, my throat suddenly too dry and constricted, "I just saw somebody become one."

I puzzled over this for the rest of the night, unable to go back to sleep (although I came to find I had only been asleep for about twenty minutes when the awful dream happened). I felt that the dream was a warning that someone was going to die on a construction site. But where? When?

About three weeks later, I had my answer. I read in the paper where in a nearby city, about ninety miles away, just such an accident had occurred: an unsecured stack of concrete pipes had broken away, crushing a construction worker to death on the work site. I was devastated. It happened almost exactly as I had dreamed it—why did I have this dream? What good is this kind of insight if you are powerless to stop anything from happening?

I actually struggled with this for years, but one day while meditating, it finally dawned on me. The epiphany I had was that basically, no matter if we *know* the future, some things are just *meant to be*... in their own time and in their own place. My bit of second sight, if you will, merely served to increase the belief in things that I just *knew* without any way of knowing, and taught me that some things you just cannot and should not change, no matter how badly you want to. In the words of Albert Einstein (paraphrasing, anyway), "God does not roll dice."

CHAPTER ELEVEN

MY GYPSY WITCH GRANDMA AND MY "SHINE"

[*A lot of people look at me like I'm kidding when I say my grandma, my mother's mother, was a gypsy witch. But she was— she really, really was. She told fortunes, using ordinary playing cards and also by the "reading" of tea leaves and coffee grounds. She also held seances, table tappings (both of which were trappings of the Spiritualism movement of the late 1800s and early 1900s), and used Ouija and other "talking" boards to make predictions and answer questions. Superstitious to a fault, my grandmother was the nearest thing to the stereotypical "holdover from the Old Country" relative that I could have ever wanted.*]

My grandmother, the same one who I will always believe was a gypsy witch, used to tell me that I had a "shine" to me. I was kinda scared of her when I was little, because, well, she *looked* like a witch, the kind you see in story books who shoves kids in ovens. So, a lot of times, whenever she told me something (about myself or otherwise), I would just smile and nod my head and try to look as sweet as possible so she wouldn't stuff me in an oven before I could figure out a way to make good my escape (as you probably have guessed, I had a strange childhood).

The whole "shine" thing came about because my grandmother, who was the only family member present in the same room during my birth (my father and brother had waited outside in the waiting area), claimed that I was born with a "veil over my face." If you've never heard of this before, don't worry—you're actually in the majority.

Being born with a "veil" (actually it's known medically as a "caul") over your face means that the amniotic sac was stretched over the head rather than being shed normally during the birthing process. It *is* considered quite rare, but more importantly, it carries a special significance—particularly in cultures where superstition is more prevalent.

Those born with a veil are claimed to have all sorts of powers and special abilities, including clairvoyance or second sight. They make excellent healers and fortune tellers supposedly, although I've never been able to pick any winning lottery numbers (kidding, sort of). In fact, I believe that the veil I was born with could possibly enhance my ability to experience paranormal events, if only for the reason that the belief in such things opens the mind to more esoteric beliefs and practices.

Since my grandmother knew about and actually saw the caul, she went hog wild when I was older about my special abilities. Much to my horror, by the time I was four or five years old, she would do her best to get me alone in her "quilting" room when we would go to visit. Here, in her darkened sewing area (which was usually off-limits to my cousins and me), she would regale me with stories of my special abilities and how I could learn how to properly grow and use my "wild talents," as Charles Fort might have written. As I stated previously, I was eager to agree with anything she said, just so that I could escape her lair and go play with my cousins who lived in houses on adjoining areas of the old farm. Sometimes, if I could repeat what she had told me successfully back to her, she would give me a prize, such as a dollar bill or Hershey bar (to this day, I find both money and chocolate to still be good motivators).

As weird as it sounds, sometimes Grandma was right —she would tell me stuff about myself that no one knew. One particular instance springs readily to mind:

On the way to her house, I'm guessing about halfway into the fifteen-mile trip, there was a farmhouse on a small rise we had to pass by. At some point prior, some young boys had been playing a game of catch in the yard. One missed catching the ball and ran down the rise after it, right out into the street, where he was struck and killed instantly by a moving car.

I can remember every time that we drove by the area, I would get a creepy, odd feeling. There were times when I'd be reading a comic book or otherwise not paying attention to the outside world at all; then I would get the odd feeling and look up to see that we were, indeed, passing the old white farmhouse on the little rise.

One particular trip to Grandma's, I had been looking out the window, counting telephone poles (this, along with counting other objects, such as mailboxes, stop signs, traffic lights, and billboards) was often a part of my traveling ritual as a child. I chalk it up to being OCD and having Asperger's), and I paid a lot of attention to the farmhouse this time. When we drove over a certain spot in the road, I knew—somehow—that this was the exact spot where the little boy had died years before. As usual, I kept these thoughts to myself, and we continued on to Grandma's house.

When we arrived and went in, my grandmother hurriedly said her hellos to my parents and then whisked me off into the quilting room. Somehow, she knew that I had experienced a much stronger encounter than usual.

She lovingly brushed my tousled hair away from my forehead, this time proffering *both* a dollar bill and a Hershey bar.

"Sometimes you feel things, don't you?" she asked as I took the money and candy from her frail, wrinkled hand. "Like that spot on the highway on the way here tonight."

My blood ran cold at her words, and I'm sure my eyes were as big as saucers. She simply smiled and clasped her hands in front of herself, satisfied. I ran as hard as I could out of the quilting room, down the hall and out the back door. She had scared the absolute crapola out of me, even worse than was usual. I seem to remember going next door to my cousin Jerry's house. I gave him the dollar bill and half of the chocolate bar—that's how creeped out I was, because under normal circumstances I would probably have figured out a way to sweet-talk him out of candy or coins. I remember thinking, *How come I have to be the one to be born with a caul over my face?* I was happy to just be left alone and to be a kid—although I realized even then that I saw and felt things other people didn't, I wasn't entirely comfortable with the idea just yet. And surprisingly, this is precisely what my grandmother *knew* and was trying to help me with coming to both terms and grips with the idea.

She also instructed me in the fine art of superstitious belief. To this day, if I see someone put a hat on the bed, it takes every bit of my very fiber not to go into an apoplectic fit. You throw a hat on a bed, you have just killed someone, just as surely if you put a gun to their head or poisoned their Cheerios or cut the brake line of their automobile. You might have even decimated a whole houseful of people. And all their livestock. Also, heaven forbid, if I crack an egg open and discover a double yolk—then you have to take that thing out and throw it over the top of the house, "lest ye bring a curse" upon the family—and if you don't think you can throw it over the house, go next door and throw it over their roof, because their house isn't as tall... I'm only partially joking here—a lot of these are real superstitions that I was forced to observe as a child.

Looking back now, I've made my peace with my gran —I forgive her for scaring me so, and I wish that now I could talk to her about all the wonderful, metaphysical things she knew and practiced on a daily basis. I was present at her deathbed when I was thirteen years old— fittingly enough, the only other time I have been in the room when someone passed away was twenty-seven years later when my mother departed. My mother claimed she had a visit from my grandma—her mother—one chilly October morning in 2002, and said that while she was silent, she looked as alive as you or I. She stepped into the doorway and looked at my mother. Their eyes met, and then the spirit of my grandma slowly backed away and was gone. My mother passed away in the hospital in October of 2003, exactly one year to the day of the visit of my grandma's apparition.

CHAPTER TWELVE

HAUNTED FAIRVIEW SCHOOL

[*A haunted school? It's not as unusual as it sounds. I suspect it's no different than, say, a haunted hospital—other than the fact that fewer people have passed away at a school. Maybe a haunted shopping mall would be a better comparison? Why would anyone want to haunt a school, you ask? Well, schools such as Columbine have a history of terrible tragedy, so that would kind of be a given. My own pet theory—and that's all it is, a theory—is that many people look back on their lives and realize (sadly, in most cases) that their school days were the happiest of all. If you could come back as a ghost, wouldn't you be drawn to a place you loved and enjoyed? Conversely, maybe you were bullied and tormented in school, and choose to come back and take vengeance in the place where you were the most miserable. Either way, haunted schools do exist. Here's my experience with the one I attended for seven years.*]

In the west Knox County community of Solway, there

stands a building that was once known as Fairview Elementary School. It was built in the early part of the last century, as part of the WPA program. I attended this school from the first through the seventh grades. The only reason I didn't attend eighth grade here was that during the summer between grades seven and eight, the school dropped grades six through eight and I was forced to go to the newly opened Karns Middle School a few miles away.

I knew right away, even as a child, that things were somewhat "different" at Fairview. I had heard from older kids, even before I started first grade, that the school was haunted. As the local playground chatter and urban legends went, it was haunted by the ghost of at least one teacher and as many as two or three kids, at least one female and one male child.

I had severe separation anxiety in the first grade. As long as my mom sat in the back of the room, I was fine—but the minute she left, I became a screaming, crying mess. I'm sure a part of it was my struggles with undiagnosed (at the time) Asperger's syndrome. I had certain little rituals that I simply had to perform at home before leaving for school, and would make sure they were completed and in the correct order, even if it made me late for school—I didn't care about being late, being late was nothing—but let me forget one little part of my "morning routine," then it was all about running back into the house and starting the process over, while my mother (bless her, she had the patience of a saint!) waited patiently in the running car, maybe honking the horn if I was really running overtime.

In addition to my OCD and Asperger tendencies, though, was the fact that the school was haunted. That didn't make it any easier. There were certain doors that opened with ease most of the time, but then would suddenly hold fast, as if being blocked on the other side. This happened not only to me, but I observed it happening to other children as well.

There were also disembodied voices, both adult and children. Voices audible to the point that the teacher would actually pause and look around the room or even go out into the hallway of the grades one to three block (three small rooms) only to find the other teachers peering out their doors into the hallway as well, with no perpetrators in sight.

Another frequent occurrence was the bell. The infamous bell—it signified the start and end of the day, as well as lunch times and the odd fire drill on occasion. The bell was located in a central point of the school, in an area where two of the three major hallways intersected. Only the principal was allowed to ring the bell, and the chain that actuated the electronic switch was safely kept high enough that curious little hands couldn't reach it. If I remember correctly, the chain was also secured to an eye hook with a little padlock to which the principal had the only key, which I remember the principal at the time, Mr. Slusher, kept on a little chain in the watch pocket of his vest.

So, here was this bell, access to which was incredibly restricted—yet at odd times it would ring—when no one was around it. It wasn't a normal ring, but rather a single "ding" that would peal throughout the school, instantly gaining the attention of all who heard it—which was everyone, being that this was a small suburban school out in the country. There was, during any given school year, about two hundred kids in the entire place. Doors would fly open, teachers would stick their heads out of the rooms, and the principal would scurry down from the office—only to find no trace of anyone near the bell. Over the seven years I was in attendance at Fairview, I saw numerous electricians, some from the county school system, others independent, check the bell's wiring, to no avail. It was just something we learned to deal with, and everyone knew that the sound of a single ding meant simply continue as you were. One redheaded kid named Robbie speculated that the single bell was an omen, and claimed that every time it happened, it meant he was going to get in trouble regarding some unrelated offense. We all nodded our heads in agreement at this idea on the playground, but I never saw any pertinent evidence to back up Robbie's claim—he had also claimed the same thing during another school year, regarding the song of a whippoorwill that had nested in a tree just outside the classroom window.

Another weird area of the school was in a narrow stairwell that led down to the school's dank musty library in the darkened basement. At the last bit of segmented hallway before entering the library proper (actually one room, about thirty feet square) was a set of doors on either side. These wooden doors, about three feet square and set about three feet up the wall, were more fabled at Fairview than the wardrobe in C. S. Lewis' book—there were tales of children entering the oddly built subbasement on either side of the hallway, never to be seen again. I know that on at least a couple of occasions I myself cracked one of the doors open on a dare and saw what inexplicably looked like one or two children crawling about in the darkness. One kid I knew named Steve brought a small battery-operated flashlight to school one day. During an opportune moment when the librarians (who would chase you away from the wooden doors if they saw you messing about) were looking away, he switched the light on and tossed it in as far as he could. Several of us peered in and saw the light, but within a couple of minutes, the dirt-walled hole was dark once more, as if the flashlight had been swallowed up by the blackness therein.

Eventually, some kid hurt themselves falling headfirst out of the door back into the hallway (it was the same Robbie from before—I wonder if the bell rang a single time before he bashed his head?) and had to be carted off in an ambulance, returning to school with seven stitches. Robbie always claimed he was shoved from behind out of the hole... But then again, he was known for wild tales and causing trouble (he and his older brother once sat in the street in front of their house, delighting in seeing how many cars they could back up in each direction). That ended not only the adventures into the doors, but the library itself. The doors were nailed and triple-padlocked shut, and the library was closed—we started getting weekly visits from the county Bookmobile. The ex-library was eventually turned into a music room, and the doors walled over with sheet rock and a fresh coat of paint, all but forgotten.

Some of my best haunted experiences at Fairview, however, were after such time as I was a student there. I hope anyone reading this will understand that this was a different time, a different era, and headlines pertaining to school violence were still decades away—but Fairview was rarely fully secured after hours. The only "security system" was either Reuben or Moses, the two elderly janitors, and they were usually out of the school and home by five or six in the evening. It was easy—very, very easy, as it were—to pay Fairview a visit after hours. I know, because, well, I paid the school such a visit on more than one occasion.

Although my mom usually drove me to school or I could choose to ride the bus, I actually lived within walking distance of the school—two miles via the roads, or a little over a mile if I went straight through the woods "as the crow flies."

On this one particular evening, it was in the fall, just about the time school was due to be back in session, my best friend John and I walked from our area over to the school. We took the roads most of the way, but cut through the fields and farmland the last half mile or so to avoid detection. While the school didn't have any security measures per se, there were watchful eyes that lived nearby—if we'd been spotted, the "Solway Grapevine," notorious for local gossip (as happens in any small community throughout the country and probably the world), would have sprung into action, and the story would have passed from mouth to ear to mouth, and our mothers would have known what we had been up to before we even made it back home.

We made it to the school undetected, and we weren't really surprised to find the doors we could get to discreetly locked tight. The windows, however, were another story. The second or third one we tried slid open noiselessly. We clambered up and lowered ourselves stealthily inside a darkened classroom in the lower grade block on the back side of the school.

The first order of business was to make sure we were truly alone—if we could slip in so easily, so could any number of people who might have decided to do so for whatever reason. We hunched silently behind a teacher's desk for what seemed like an eternity, but was probably all of fifteen or twenty minutes. Other than the usual creaks and groans associated with a building from the 1930s with some hardwood flooring, we were greeted with an eerie silence.

This eerie silence I'm speaking of—it pervades the mind regarding places we usually consider very noisy. If you've ever been in a school or a church or a shopping mall or an amusement park—and you're the only one there—then you know just how creepy the silence is of which I write. It gives the place a reverence that it might not otherwise deserve...

So here we were, skulking around in our old elementary school, eyes accustomed to the darkness. We kept low going by the doors and windows and kept a wary eye out for any telltale headlights in the parking area or the sounds that one of the heavy wooden doors might make if being unlocked. We weren't here to do anything more than explore and bask in the thrill of being in this particular circumstance.

We went from classroom to classroom, recalling time previously spent in each one. Some bad, some good—but all youthful nostalgia now, even though John and I had only been out of the school one and two years, respectively. The office was locked, so we didn't proceed any further in that regard—if it was locked inside the school building proper, we meant for it to remain that way. We even dared each other to go into the girls' room, which we did—penetrating that wonder of wonders that we barely understood at that time. I can remember marveling at the vending machines on the wall and only having the slightest idea of what they were for, although John—having grown up with three older sisters—had a better idea than I about those strange coin-operated boxes bolted to the wall. Ah, youth, when so many things were a mystery!

After the foray into forbidden territory, we decided to end our trip into the unknown by visiting the combination auditorium/gym/lunchroom down at the lower end of the campus. This would be our final destination that evening and had a convenient side door well hidden from any casually observing neighbor or random passerby. We walked down the seven or so steps into the sunken area and as silently as possible opened one of the large wooden double doors that led into the cavernous space.

While our eyes had become accustomed to the darkness in the hallways of the school, there was enough ambient light coming into the hallway windows from outside to allow us to see. The gym was a different story —there were wire-mesh-covered windows set way up high near the ceiling as the sole natural light source. The moon was full at the time or very near it, and it could be seen shining brightly in those high windows and sending a shaft of light across the gym at an angle. Thanks to the brightness of the moon, the other areas of the huge room were cast in inky darkness. We stood just inside the doors, gazing into the velvety black abyss—when we heard it.

It started slowly at first and then became faster. It was the unmistakable click-click, click-click, click-click of a pair of high-heeled women's shoes crossing the gym. As the pace quickened, the clicking grew louder, and there was no mistaking it was heading straight for us—however, the shaft of moonlight perfectly lit the area where the footsteps were coming from—and there was absolutely no one there. As the click-clicks became maddeningly, insanely close, whatever paralysis we suffered suddenly broke, and we dashed back through the wooden doors, up the stairs in a single bound, and out one of the front doors of the school in a dead run. I don't think we looked back until we were across the field that would lead us safely away from the area.

We collapsed in the high grass, panting, drawing in deep whooping breaths of the chill night air. After catching our breath, we flopped over and just observed the school and surrounding area for a bit. Thankfully, we hadn't been spotted by the school's neighbors when fleeing. No lights came on in any part of the school either, further enforcing the fact that we had just come face-to-face (almost) with one of the more prominent legends of the school—the Phantom Teacher.

The story of the Phantom Teacher had been told

almost as long as the school had been there. My mom hadn't heard it in the 1930s, but the school was new then. By the time my brother started first grade there in 1951, the tale was already in full swing. The legend was that a certain teacher had died in the school (mercifully after the children had left for the day) and her spirit remained trapped in the school. Other variations included her being killed in a car accident on the way home, or simply retiring and coming back to haunt the school in her afterlife. Other than the last scenario, I was unable to find any information about a teacher having died while still teaching, and the remaining bit of the legend makes the most sense in an Occam's razor sort of way.

We're both sure of what we heard and *didn't* see. We made other forays into the school, most of which were later on after the campus had closed completely and had been vandalized and trashed by the locals who were less respectful than we had been. There were no paranormal events on those occasions—perhaps the sad state of the school had forced the ghost to go elsewhere for another school to haunt. Instead of being demolished, a tech company stepped up and bought the property and revamped it into the current Fairview Technology Center facility. Are there ghosts there now? Who knows? I suppose one could ask the scientists who work there if they've ever experienced anything strange, but by the very nature of being scientists, they may not believe in such things as haunted elementary schools. Please bear in mind, however, this facility is a highly surveilled, very private property now and should be respected as such, although I have included pertinent information below, just in case anyone would like to possibly pursue further paranormal research—one never knows—they might consider a lockdown and paranormal investigation as something fun to do...

[Fairview Technology Center is located at 11020 Solway School Rd., Knoxville, TN 37931. For a gallery of recent photos, visit:

http://www.knoxdevelopment.org/BusinessIncubator/Fairview-Gallery.aspx]

CHAPTER THIRTEEN

BEAVER RIDGE CEMETERY

[Beaver Ridge Cemetery is located at the corner of Copper Ridge Road and Emory Road in Knoxville, Tennessee. The cemetery is in west Knox County, near the Karns community. Although the cemetery is public property and anyone can visit, I ask that any of my readers exercise caution and respect. Please be aware that many of the families in the surrounding area have loved ones and other kinfolk buried there, and may not take kindly to interloping strangers. Be it also known that the Knox County Sheriff's Department steps up their patrols of the area after dark, and especially on Halloween and the nights leading up to the spooky holiday.]

Now I want to make certain that anyone reading this understands just exactly *which* Copper Ridge I'm talking about, as there are *two* so-named areas that have seen more than their share of weird activity. This is BEAVER Ridge Cemetery, on COPPER Ridge ROAD. There is (or was) a Copper Ridge CHURCH in another part of town, where glowing crosses could be seen in the windows overlooking the parking area. Due to all the publicity and rubberneckers, that church has since changed its name and no longer welcomes visitors who come just to see the glowing crosses. It also doesn't help in reducing confusion that Beaver Ridge Cemetery used to have an old abandoned (and supposedly, very haunted) building right next to it, that had been at one time a church, among other things (such as an elementary school and a Masonic lodge), and the church's address was... Copper Ridge Road. If you're still unclear, email me for more details (as always, my contact details, including email address, can be found at the end of this book).

The cemetery I am referring to is at the corner of Copper Ridge Road and Emory Road in Knox County Tennessee, just outside the Karns community. The *REAL* name of the cemetery is *Beaver Ridge Cemetery* (and apparently has been since 1815, according to the nice bricked sign that's been added in recent years), but we always called it Copper Ridge Cemetery because it's on Copper Ridge *Road*. Karns folks will know what I'm talking about if I say go to the red light, keep going past the turn to the old high school, and then take a right at the old Orris Lynch place—the cemetery will be just up the road on the right...

But I digress. Ever since I was just a little tadpole attending kindergarten at the Karns Methodist Church, I heard about the cemetery and accompanying school/church/building being haunted. I went to grade school in the Solway community at Fairview Elementary (see the whole chapter dedicated to it), a couple of miles away from Karns, so I didn't hear much about Copper Ridge Cemetery from the first through the seventh grade. But, let me tell you, from the day I first started eighth grade at Karns Middle (and all four years after at Karns High), I heard the oft-repeated tales over and over again.

My friend Kenny reportedly saw someone in Victorian garb walking around in the cemetery after dark. On another occasion, he saw some dark figure stabbing a knife into a grave repeatedly. I had no reason not to believe Kenny, as he lived within easy walking distance of the cemetery and was also the toughest kid I knew—being small of stature and being blessed/cursed with strong opinions and no brain-to-mouth filter, Kenny had grown up tough, often using his fists to prove a point. Thankfully, I never had to fight him—it would have been akin to fighting a wild cat with a buzzsaw. I saw Kenny take on groups of three or four guys all bigger than him and come out victorious. So, if a true playground badass like Kenny told you about something that *scared* even him, then that was all the endorsement I required to give the tale adequate weight.

Plus, it wasn't just Kenny I heard the stories from. It was a whole slew of kids—even their parents and in some cases grandparents got into the act. In the Karns community, Copper Ridge Cemetery was a legendary place.

My first visit was one day after classes were over in high school. I was going home with my friend Will after school to look at his new hunting rifle, and I happened to mention the cemetery as we drove past. He turned onto Copper Ridge Road, then parked in a small gravel turnout on the side of the street opposite Copper Ridge Cemetery, where there just happens to be *another* cemetery (although I've heard differently, I think it's part of the same cemetery, but just on the other side of Copper Ridge Road).

It was a stormy, windy day, so it was the perfect daylight introduction to the cemetery. Will and I got out and walked around between the stones. I recognized many Karns family names and luminaries. In front of the cemetery, right on the edge of Emory Road, was an old building. It was one of those old buildings that just look haunted. Growing up (well, during middle school and high school, anyway), I had heard that the building was haunted. Of all the different stories, I heard the following: it was a school, it was a church, it was the home of a secret society. Well, all three are actually true. It started out as a church, was later used as a school (in the 1930s, when my mom was attending Fairview, she knew kids who attended (I suppose the name was Copper Ridge *School*). And, last but not least, when my father first became a Mason and started attending lodge meetings, his group met in the old building until the Beaver Ridge Lodge on nearby Oak Ridge Highway was completed. Again, the fact that it had been all three things that I had heard it had been, this lent credence to the building being haunted. Plus, like I stated earlier, the place just *looked* haunted…

Peering in the dusty windows (at the time, the building had been closed down for years and wasn't used for anything, but was still intact with doors and windows and in overall generally good shape), I half expected to see shadows flitting around. Standing back in the cemetery, the upstairs windows facing the graveyard were even creepier, like you were being watched by some unseen entity inside the building. I had even heard one tale of an enterprising lad who had snuck a tape recorder into the building one night, pressed the "record" button and then snuck away. When he returned the next morning and retrieved the recorder, he was so horrified at what he had captured on the tape—howls, shrieks, screams, whispers, chants and other assorted and sundry voices and sounds—that he immediately erased the tape and vowed to never set foot in either the old church/school or cemetery again.

As stated, these kinds of tales were plentiful—it seems that anyone and everyone in the Karns community had at least one story of their own personal experience they could tell, and knew of a couple of dozen more first-hand accounts they had heard from family and friends. It seems that older brothers and sisters (or sometimes cousins) had the best stories to relate when it came to the strange goings-on in Beaver Ridge Cemetery.

So, even though my first introduction to the area was mild, it would get better. There was a storm blowing in out of the west, over Black Oak Ridge, and my friends suggested we might not want to be among the trees and headstones during a real boom-banger of an electrical storm. I agreed, and we retreated to his house in the Camelot subdivision just a bit farther up Emory Road, with the understood, unspoken promise that we would return soon to check it out at night. I particularly wanted to see if the stories about how some of the stones glowed in the dark were true.

Sure enough, a few weeks later, we had a long weekend off from school coming up. What better way to alleviate the rigors and boredom of high school academia than with hanging out in a haunted graveyard? I was all about it and could barely wait until Friday arrived.

Friday night found us at my friend Will's house, packing for a "ghost-hunting expedition"—about thirty years before such things as are now commonly broadcast as "reality TV." We gathered up our gear (which was really just a couple of flashlights, a Sony microcassette recorder, pocketknives and, for added a protection, an ancient bolt-action, single-shot .22 rifle, which we stashed in the trunk by itself (truth be told, the old rifle was a relic and was probably more dangerous to the person trying to fire it than the person being fired upon). Thankfully, the rifle remained in the trunk throughout the night, as we parked our vehicle at the high school and walked the half mile or so back to Beaver Ridge Cemetery, lest someone spot our car parked right beside the cemetery (as most explorers did and usually got busted).

When we arrived at the cemetery, the first thing we did was walk the perimeter and make sure we were the only people (living, anyway) in attendance on that particular night. Pleased and satisfied that we were all alone, we set about fanning out among the stones and walking a grid, to see if we could stir up any paranormal activity.

Dressed head to toe in black, if anyone had spotted us in the cemetery that night (and they may well have), they would have assumed we were some sort of dark wraiths up to no good (probably not far from the truth, also).

I did notice that when the moon was just right, some of the stones did seem to give off a pearlescent glow; however, I think this was actually flecks of perhaps mica or quartz in the giant granite headstones that caught enough of the ambient light to cast a glow.

We made a couple of passes near the back side of the cemetery, where it was rumored that an easily riled caretaker armed with a shotgun loaded with rock salt lived, praying for the nights when he managed to catch interlopers in his cemetery.

Sure enough, there was an old run-down mobile home back there, the sole window flickering with what was most likely a black-and-white television. We carefully backtracked and swung a huge loop around the cemetery in the other direction away from the trailer, figuring there was no use in pushing our luck.

Shortly after midnight, we saw headlights turn onto Copper Ridge Road, and a Ford station wagon (one of the huge road boats from the early 1970s, with simulated wood grain paneling down the sides) pulled into the little gravel area and doused its lights and engine quickly. We lay flat on the ground and belly crawled over behind some large stones for cover as we got a better look.

In a few minutes, we saw a flashlight playing over the area, and peeked from our hiding spot to observe a strange beast—it appeared to have about eight or ten arms, the same amount of legs, and four or five hairy heads... What we were seeing was actually a group of girls, cheerleaders from our high school, no less, pressed together so closely that they resembled the horrific beast I described above as they slid along the far edge of the graveyard.

I turned to my friend and even in the dark could see he was grinning ear to ear. I flashed him a thumbs-up, knowing that fortune had smiled upon us this evening. We were about to scare the pants off some of our classmates!

Since we were dressed in black, it was no problem to move around stealthily. The only thing we had to remember was to keep low and not get caught with any light behind us that might give us away in silhouette. Will, thinner and more limber than me, silently pulled himself up into the low-hanging branches of a cedar tree, while I picked an excellent dark spot nearby in the shadow of a giant memorial headstone. We waited silently, holding our collective breath.

Shortly, the group came nearer to where we had hidden ourselves. I heard their breathless voices get closer and closer, until I could finally make out what they were saying. The main girl, the "ringleader" I'll call her (I won't name names, because I'm sure any in the group would love to get ahold of me to this day), was saying how silly it was to be scared here. After all, it was just an old cemetery, and what was there to be afraid of anyway and...

... and just then Will dropped from his perch in the tree, not more than a half dozen feet in front of the group. You've never heard such a scream in your life! Just as they found their feet and turned to run, I sprang from my hiding place with a loud, low moan. Suddenly the "many-limbed monster" split into five very scared girls, who were now running willy-nilly, hell-bent on escaping the cemetery alive. As Will and I watched them run away, we turned along the tree line to hide in the edge of the woods until they were gone. As we made our way, Will elbowed me in the ribs and pointed. Behind the girls and off to the right a bit, another dark figure gave chase, eliciting even more screams.

"Who the heck is that?" I whispered as we both dropped out of sight in the tall grass. "Did you tell anyone else we were going to be here tonight?"

Will swore that he hadn't, and I knew that I hadn't. We saw the station wagon burst to life, reverse out of the spot, and then vanish, heading west into the darkness onto Emory Road in a cloud of dust and thrown gravel.

We held our position in the high weeds for a good thirty minutes, waiting for the other "scary" person to reveal themselves. Oddly enough, we never caught sight of anyone, even when we eventually came out of hiding and stealthily looked over the entire cemetery and surrounding area. We finally headed back to our parking spot at the high school and then on to Will's house a little after two in the morning, beat, dirty, sweaty, tired and mystified. We made our bunks in Will's basement, vowing to go back the next day, Saturday, in broad daylight and see what we could see. All night, I dreamed of being in the cemetery and of being chased by a dark "boogeyman" with no face. I kind of felt this was well-deserved karma for having given the cheerleaders a fright they would never forget. The next morning I woke up groggy from all the commotion the night before, and stiff from sleeping on the floor of Will's dad's basement study in my sleeping bag.

Will and I dragged ourselves upstairs, where his mom had a full breakfast of eggs, bacon, sausage, hash browns, toast, orange juice and black coffee (ahh, yes) waiting for us. After the feast, we had energy to spare and decided we would just jog the mile or so to the cemetery from this location. An excellent plan.

In the light of day, the Beaver Ridge Cemetery is not as scary as in the literal dead of night—but it does have a certain feel about it, that while many cemeteries also have, not all do—I would almost describe it as a feeling of extreme sadness, an overwhelming sense of pathos, if you will indulge me. It's almost as if the graves, each and every one of them, are speaking out to you, the living—not in an audible language, but a language, a patois if you will, of post-human that is more felt than heard, but speaks volumes to the hearer, nonetheless. It gives one a new perspective on life and death and mortality. Did these people want to die? Were they ready to shuffle off this mortal coil? I would wager that not one in a hundred of the people in any given cemetery are truly ready to make that journey, to see what lies beyond the thin veil—as thin as a single breath—between this life and the great beyond. There is unfinished business—words not yet spoken, apologies unmade, songs unsung, tales untold—this is the language of the dead... Part of the reason that I became a writer and chronicler of folklore and stories and tall tales and myths and legends and things that go bump in the night is due to an epiphany I had at the funeral of my maternal grandmother (yes, the very same one I had feared as a child, because I thought she looked like a witch), and because she told me of the wild talents that I *surely* must possess, because I was born with a veil over my face and...

As I stood there looking down at her in her coffin, all eighty-nine pounds of her withered hull, I observed the silence of her lips, the stillness of her hands. I thought about all the stories she had told me in my youth, many of which scared the dickens out of me, no doubt scarring me for life—and I realized that those tales died with her. As her words faded and echoed into the mists of time, no longer would I hear a cautionary tale about going mad if a dog bit me during the "dog days" of summer. Or most likely having to have my foot—nay, my entire leg amputated (and that was if I was lucky) should I be so foolish and unfortunate as to step into the morning dew on the grass and, unknowingly, have a cut on my foot—"dew poisoning" was swift and sure and merciless and there was no cure.

Well, maybe some of those stories needed to die—but I chose at that moment in time not to let them. Not just the stories of my grandmother, but of my aunts and uncle and parents and friends of the family and old toothless men who sat on rotting porches covered with rusty screen and spun their tales of terror and of lessons learned. I would be the scribe to record these tales, so that they might last not only longer than those who told them, but longer than those who heard them as well. I had found my purpose in life... But I digress.

So here we were in this cemetery in broad daylight,

before noon even, and it still had a spooky, scary, creepy feel. You always hear people describe it as "I felt as if I were being watched." Well, that was exactly what it felt like. Perhaps it was the dark canopy of old-growth cedar trees that lined the back of the graveyard. Or maybe the ever-present hollow-eyed stare of the darkened windows of the old abandoned school/church/masonic hall. Or maybe the high grass that ringed three sides of the property. Or the fact that from where the cemetery stood, you couldn't see any houses or people or any living thing, save for the odd crow or two that occasionally took wing over the stones, cawing, taunting. Even the wind seemed different on top of the small knob—it would come up out of nowhere and whip your hair and clothing around you and moan through the trees when you were in certain parts of the cemetery.

We ventured over and peeked inside the old building as best we could from outside, the windows and doors long since vanished through time or neglect or vandalism. It wasn't that we were scared to enter the building because of ghosts or witches or Satanists or any of the other myriad things we'd heard were lurking inside, but rather the old wooden floorboards even on the ground floor were rotting away—I shudder to think what the stairs and upper floors might have looked like based on these perilous conditions. Contented that there were not any ghosts or witches or Satanists hiding inside, we traced a lazy route around the entire perimeter of the cemetery. We could see where we had hidden the night before, the tall grass still mashed down and bearing witness to our having lain there as we'd watched the other figure, as dark as night and oh so nimble, frolic amongst the stones. We even went and checked the spot where Will had clambered up into the tree and where I had crouched behind the squat, rectangular obelisk bearing the "Garrison" family name. We checked all the angles and figured that whatever we had seen would surely have been able to see us, especially before we were made known to its presence. I felt goosebumps rise on my arms even in the warm morning sun, as I imagined some dark wraith curiously watching us from a distance and then deciding to join in on the fun when we had popped out to frighten the hapless group of cheerleaders. What did we see? We truly did not then or now, thirty years or more in the future, have any idea who—or what —decided to join us on that night.

We searched in the area where the dark figure had come from, but couldn't find a trace of anything. There were no footprints, no cigarette butts or gum wrappers, or any sign of where it had lain in the tall grass and waited as we had. Whatever it was, it must have been from nearby, although the sheer logistical impossibility of this notion at the time cannot be stressed strongly enough. Even today, with the advent of Google Maps, you can see that there is not much close by—and there was even less those thirty plus years ago.

Although a tiny bit scared, we were more curious than frightened. We decided, for reasons of scientific exploration and posterity, that we would return that night. We would arrive a good half hour or so before dark, in order to walk a grid of the cemetery and surrounds to fully ensure we were the only ones present.

Satisfied with our plan, we jogged back to Will's house to ponder and wait and plot.

After what seemed like an eternity—I'm sure all of eight or nine hours—we decided it was time to return to the cemetery. Once again, we drove down to the high school (which is now the elementary school) and parked Will's car. And also once again, we were dressed in black from head to toe, black anti-glare football player makeup smeared on our faces. I'm sure we were quite the sight. This time though, since it was still daylight, we decided to duck behind the high school, find a place to ford Beaver Creek, and be in the creek bottom across from the cemetery in a fraction of the time it would have taken to sneak along the highway and risk being spotted and, heaven forbid, have to explain to a curious adult or skeptical law enforcement officer just exactly what we were doing sneaking around in these otherwise ridiculous getups.

We acted like we were on a combat mission and were able to sneak past and behind the high school without being spotted. I'm sure that Frank West or one of the other janitorial staff was in the building, but we were fast and wily and camouflaged. In as much as getting past and behind the high school was no problem, fording Beaver Creek presented a whole other set of circumstances. In the low bottoms, which began just behind the school, the ground was at best soft and muddy and at worst dotted with deep puddles and pockets of quicksand-like mud that liked to do funny things, like suck the shoes off your very feet. We spent the better part of thirty minutes walking up and down the banks of the creek, trying to find a place where we could just walk across. Will and I both knew of such places, but—unfortunately—they would have required us walking several miles out of our way, and they were also in areas where there were houses and farms and dogs and other assorted and sundry things that would make it easier for us to get caught. So we gathered our courage, stripped off our socks, shoes and pants—and waded across Beaver Creek in our underwear.

I've been in some cold water before, but I've never felt water as cold as it was in Beaver Creek that afternoon as the sun began to dip low behind the trees. We're talking take-your-breath-away cold, and I'm sure I speak for Will also when I say that I'm glad the water only came up to mid-thigh rather than our waists. We hurriedly chicken-walked through the creek and hurriedly put our pants and socks and shoes back on as we stood shivering just above the bank of the creek. Time was of the essence—even though it would have been hard to explain all the black clothing and grease-paint, being practically bare-assed out in the woods would have brought a whole new level of eyebrow raising from any interested parties.

We hid in the tall grass on the right-of-way by Emory Road. For a usually unbusy stretch of rural road, it seemed particularly busy that day. Cars, trucks, people pulling boats, Orris Lynch on a tractor—we had a parade of traffic in both directions there for a bit. Fortunately, the coast finally cleared, and we darted out of the ditch, across Emory Road, and into another ditch just below the school/church/masonic lodge. The only thing left was to escape the prying eyes of the possible caretaker who lived in a run-down mobile home off to our left. As we scurried up the bank and finally entered the cemetery proper, I heard a dog "woof" curiously a couple of times, but then it went silent. We had made it!

As planned, we regrouped and then set about skulking along the edges of the perimeter to see if we had any unexpected company already in hiding. I doubted as much, as I didn't think anyone else would be as dedicated (or foolish, as a matter of opinion) to already be out in the cemetery when it was easily a half hour before twilight. It was dark under the trees though, and the high grass around the sides provided adequate cover as twilight approached. After thoroughly checking the grounds—we had saved the building for last—we were reasonably sure that we were quite alone in our quest to conquer the Ghosts of Beaver Ridge Cemetery. Seriously though, we were committed—or crazy—or both.

We walked the perimeter one last time before taking our places in the high grass in the back of the cemetery. We felt this was better than hiding in the tree and behind the headstone, respectively, as we had done the previous night. We settled in for the night. Unless something really, really strange and scary went down, we were here for the duration—meaning all night long, if that was what it took.

The first few hours, as expected, were mind-numbingly boring. It wasn't until midnight or thereabouts that things began to liven up—pardon the expression. Out of the corner of his eye, Will thought that he had seen a light in the old abandoned building. While sneakily making our way over to check it out, I managed to scare some sort of bird that was nesting in the low branch of a cedar tree. It gave a deafening squawk and flew off into the night. It took every ounce of my fiber to hold my ground (and not shriek as well) when I disturbed the bird, but as I saw it fly away, I realized what it was. Relieved, at least regarding the tree-dwelling shrieking night bird, we inched closer to the old building. I went in one direction toward the front, and Will went in the other. We thought that if someone was observing us and tried to make a run for it, at least one of us would stand a good chance of spotting the perpetrator. No dice, though—we met in front of the building with no incident to report. Perhaps the shrieking bird had alerted anyone inside to our presence, and they were lying low in the building. We had already decided there was no way we were going to go into the abandoned structure, especially at night. We had no desire to break a leg, if lucky, or a neck (and become yet another ghost on the premises) if we crashed through the upper floor.

As we carefully slipped back around the building, this time it was my turn to catch something from the corner of my eye... just as we cleared the area between the building and the start of the cemetery proper, I thought I saw someone, possibly a small child from the size and shape of the figure, duck behind one of the giant marble headstones. I grabbed Will's elbow and we dropped to the ground, prone. I quietly informed him of what I had seen, and pointed out the general area. I told him to watch near the back and side of the cemetery, and I would make for the stone where I thought the kid was hiding. Will nodded silently in agreement, and we stood, half crouching, and ran toward the stone.

As we approached the headstone in question, I rose to my full height and began walking slowly. I motioned to Will to take the right side, and I took the left. I slipped a small but powerful flashlight from the pocket of my black hoodie. I stepped around the stone and flicked the pencil-thin beam on simultaneously—and there was no sign of anything.

I shrugged my shoulders at Will and flicked the light beam off. I knew that I had spotted something—I'd seen its blackened silhouette as it ducked behind the stone. I suppose that it could have ducked behind other stones besides that one, managing to keep out of our line of sight. It was possible, but highly improbable. We stealthily made our way back to the rear edge of the tall grass and once again concealed ourselves therein. We sat and waited.

About one in the morning, we saw a similar situation as the night before begin to take place. This time, instead of a station wagon with wood-grain paneling, a dusty orange Chevy van pulled into the gravel parking turnout on the other side of Copper Ridge Road. Once again, a set of girls came sneaking across the road, flashlight in hand. We didn't understand exactly what we were observing—a vehicle load of cheerleaders, two nights in a row? The only thing we could figure was that this was some sort of "initiation" that the varsity girls' squad was making the junior girls endure. Either way, it was win-win for us. We might have the opportunity to scare some of our classmates (or at least see them being scared by something else); plus we might get another chance to see whatever the strange shape was that had helped us chase the crew from the previous night. We slowly crept into our positions from the night before—Will silently lifted himself up into the massive cedar, and I crouched behind the rectangular stone that marked the Garrison family plot.

I was in place and ready to go when I heard Will slip down from his perch in the tree. He sidled up to me and said something along the lines of, "These are cheerleaders from our high school. Normally, they wouldn't give us the time of day—why are we trying to frighten them off, exactly?"

I had to admit, he had me there. They probably still wouldn't give us the time of day, but it was at least worth a shot. We turned on our penlights and started toward the group, who were gathered on the edge of the cemetery and so pressed together that they looked like one giant, misshapen girl. Tonight was going to be interesting after all.

We got the girls' attention and managed not to scare them away. It seems that there is safety in numbers, after all. Other than the mysterious glow that does indeed come from some of the tombstones when the weather and other conditions are just right, we didn't really experience anything out of the ordinary that night—unless you count Will and I having two cheerleaders on each arm, pressed close and holding on for dear life. Ah, youth...

Later in life, I have paid the occasional solo visit to Beaver Ridge Cemetery, both in the daytime and in the dead of night. Sadly, the old church/school/masonic hall has been demolished, although pictures of it still exist on the internet. I had always hoped that someone would buy the property from the county and restore it for its significant historical value, but alas—it wasn't to be.

In my twenties, I had one of the most intense episodes of déjà vu I have ever encountered. I had driven past the cemetery and was passing a farm. The moon was full and bright, the night sky cloudless. I suddenly was flooded with a memory from childhood that flashed over and over in my mind. I turned around several times and re-drove the route over and over. I wasn't able to shake the weird feeling, nor could I ever explain it—it is as if the whole area on Copper Ridge Road has an aura of mystery to it.

Another friend once told me of a nudist camp hidden in the woods off Copper Ridge Road. A little further investigation proved that the camp was actually a Christian teen summer camp and that my friend was very liberal with what he considered the "truth." Although he did finally admit that, okay, it's not a nudist camp per se, he did witness a handful of people playing volleyball in the buff. Okay, Paul, sure you did...

As I stated in the forward blurb at the beginning of this chapter, anyone is free to visit Beaver Ridge Cemetery and to drive up and down Copper Ridge Road—but please be respectful. If you do see or experience anything in this location, I'd love to hear from you. As always, my contact information can be found at the end of this volume.

CHAPTER FOURTEEN

THE HAUNTED PHOTOGRAPH

[I have always had the firm belief that just like houses or bars or office buildings or places in the woods, inanimate objects can be haunted as well. We see this, often in simple representations of people (i.e., Key West's famous "Robert the Doll," and the haunted "Annabelle" doll in the Warren's extensive hauntings research). This story is about a haunted photograph I experienced as a child.]

When I was young, sometimes when my mom would pick me up from school, we would drop by and visit an elderly friend of hers whom I only knew as Mrs. Fox.

Mrs. Fox was an ancient woman, at least it seemed so to the six-year-old me. At the time I would have guessed she was well over a hundred years old (no doubt she was actually in her late eighties or early nineties at the time). My mom had known Mrs. Fox since she was younger than I was at the time, a fact that seemed impossible to my young mind. Did people really live to be that old? She reminded me of one of the people in the Bible, from the Old Testament, who lived hundreds of years.

However, even though she seemed old enough to have remembered when the wheel was invented, she was as sweet as pie to me, always ready to tell me a story or fill my jacket pocket full of homemade cookies or other little—yet personal and meaningful—gifts.

I remember on one visit, I was proudly showing her a tiny penknife my father had recently given me. She admired it, but made me promise I'd be careful and not cut, stab or slash myself or any other children. After I'd promised eagerly to be careful with my little weapon, she smiled broadly, her timeless eyes sparkling, and said she had some presents for me. I was ecstatic, as usual—even though I was totally spoiled as a child, I was always appreciative of any gift, especially from such a wonderful woman as Mrs. Fox.

She left me sitting at her little kitchen table and in a few moments returned from the back of her house with a bundle tied with string in one hand and a small paper sack in the other. The paper sack was folded over and had a small ribbon attached.

As I had already surmised, the paper sack contained some of her homemade peanut butter cookies (my favorite!), but the other small parcel was what kept my rapt attention. She asked me to please wait until I got home to open it, but told me it was some ephemera she had been saving for me. (She was the first person I had ever heard use that word, of course—she not only explained what it meant to me, but also helped me learn to pronounce it—at school, I was the only first grader who could proudly state that he "collected ephemera" and know what he was talking about.)

I kept my promise and didn't untie the bundle until after we had arrived back at home. The "ephemera" she had proudly bestowed upon me was truly an interesting and unusual collection. All of the items were paper of some form or another. There were clippings from the newspaper, mostly cartoon panels, but some photographs or interesting articles and even a few recipes. There were also some postcards sent from her various family members. There were also some little handmade notecards with little poems or inspirational verses on them, which I recognized as being lettered in Mrs. Fox's slow, steady and even block printing.

Also in the batch of paper bits were some black-and-white photos. Wallet-sized snapshots of about a dozen or so kids, all very foreign appearing. I asked my mother about this in particular, as I wasn't sure why Mrs. Fox would have pictures of small children from other countries. My mother glanced briefly at the photos and said it was probably due to Mrs. Fox's philanthropic nature. Although far from rich, she had been left very well off financially and often gave money to the poor and underprivileged. My mother further explained that (at the time, before Sally Struthers sought donations on television) it was common for child relief agencies throughout the world to send pictures of poor and or orphaned children to prospective donors. In theory, one could conceivably pick out the little boys and or little girls that would be the recipients of charitable donations. The explanation soothed my curiosity, so I retreated back to my "study" (actually a corner of my bedroom where I had stuck an old rolltop desk next to the bookshelf I referred to as my "library") and began sorting through the collection and planning on what I was going to do with all the fascinating pieces.

While looking through the pictures of the orphaned and needy kids, however, I came across a picture that disturbed me. It was of a little boy, probably not much older than myself. It was hard to determine where he might have been from, as he had seemingly both Asiatic and Hispanic features. Unlike the majority of the other photos, his listed no country of origin on the back. He had a spiky, buzz-cut head full of dark hair and was wearing a little checkered button-up shirt with a plain white tee underneath. But the thing that was the most striking was his eyes and the expression on his face. To this day, if I close my eyes and let my memory carry me back, I can still see those piercing black eyes and the pinched little scowl on his tiny face. It was a look of something between desperate evil and sheer terror. I knew nothing of such topics at the time, but if I had to guess now, I would hazard that the boy had seem some horrible forms of the worst kind of abuse—and it had made him into some sort of monster. The photo literally gave my six-year-old self shivers as I examined the boy's contorted face, and it felt if those tiny dark coals of eyes were searing into my very soul. I had to keep the photo facedown lest it upset me worse than it already had.

As I continued to sort the rest of the collection—including the photos of the other children, which were nice and not scary in the least—I would occasionally flip the photo over and stare at it as long as I could, which wasn't very long, before flipping it over again. It was not unlike a moth being drawn to a flame—I was terrified of the boy, but couldn't help looking at the photo over and over, perhaps trying to put a finger on just what it was about the photo that scared me so.

Remembering back, I think it was the dark eyes that scared me. They seem to be devoid of all color, even though it was a black-and-white photograph—it was as if the very sclerae, the "whites of his eyes," were black. The only eyes I've ever seen a picture of that were so dark and haunting were those of convicted child murderer Andrew Pixley I saw once in a documentary, where the narrator and person being interviewed talked about how dark the killer's eyes were.

After a couple of hours of scaring myself regarding how scary the photo was, I calmly took it and put it in our kitchen garbage, which was actually contained in a large paper bag from a supermarket. Back in those days, in the mid/late 1960s, eastern Tennessee was rural enough that there wasn't any trash pickup. In the area we resided in, west Knox County, we had the option of hauling our garbage to different dumps, each about seven miles away, or burning it in a cinder-block pit in our backyard. Just for ease and convenience, like all of our neighbors, we elected to burn the trash.

So, with that taken care of, the picture of the scary child with the evil eyes put away, I was free to continue my project with the remaining bits of ephemera. As far as I can remember, I pasted the bulk of them into the odd dozen or so scrapbooks I kept as a child. Long lost to the mists of time, I would love to have a look into these today, perhaps to get a better idea of my Asperger's and OCD self at that young and tender age. Part of being an "Aspie" (probably the best part) meant never being bored—I could sit for hours (and often did) sorting articles from the paper, note cards, wallpaper samples, comic strips and the like into huge themed volumes.

I had forgotten all about the photo and easily a couple of weeks had gone by. At that time, we burned our garbage at least once a week, sometimes twice, so the photo of the frightening child was no longer in my realm of interest. I was happily reading some comic books on the floor of our living room and decided to go fix myself something to eat. As was my habit, I carefully slid the small stack of comics, the one I was reading on top and folded open to my spot, underneath the duvet skirt along the bottom edge of the couch, near the right front leg. This way, I knew precisely where the comic books were, and I didn't have to worry about them getting stepped on or put away by my mother (I distinctly remember my father being at work at the time).

I came back shortly with whatever I had found to snack on (probably pork skins, a perennial childhood favorite of mine) and, reassuming my position on the floor in front of the television with some throw pillows, reached underneath the edge of the sofa to retrieve my carefully hidden comics.

The first thing I noticed was that the top comic, which I had purposely left open, was closed and stacked on top of the rest. While I remember thinking it was odd, I wasn't really disturbed. Strange things happen sometimes, I guess. It was about to get even stranger...

I flipped through the top comic, looking for where I had previously left off—when I gasped. The photo of the scary little boy—which I had put in the trash weeks ago—was looking back at me from inside the comic book! I cried out and swatted the photo away, as if it were a bug or spider—as far as I was concerned, it was worse than that. The flick of my hand caught the photo just so, and it flew back under the edge of the couch, perfectly into the tiny crack between the edge of the duvet cover and the floor. I sighed. I wasn't going to let it bother me now, although it had already frightened me out of my wits by at least half. I went back to my coveted snack and my comic book, choosing to ignore the silly idea that the photograph had "returned from the dead" of being burned in our trash heap.

After I had finished, I started to shove the comic stack back under the couch for later perusal, but I knew something had to be done about the photo that was hidden in my comic book hiding spot. I pinched the edge of the duvet cover tightly between my thumb and index finger and gingerly lifted it up as I peeked underneath the couch—I was still frightened of the photo enough that there was no way I was going to stick my hand under there, into that dark place. I didn't see anything other than some small trinkets (probably Cracker Jack toys—this was back in the day when they still put tiny toys in the boxes, instead of a sticker or some such claptrap). Undaunted, I went into the utility room to retrieve one of the large flashlights my father always kept around.

Returning, I plopped back on the floor, clicked on the light, and flipped up the edge of the duvet cover. As I played the beam around under the couch, I was kind of surprised not to see the photo... and then all of a sudden, there it was—propped against the square wooden pillar of the couch leg, those blacker-than-black eyes staring back at me from underneath the couch...

I shrieked and drew back a bit. I mean, sure, it could just so happen that when I flicked the photo, it had stood up on end... Yeah, of course... The selfsame photo that had somehow escaped from the grocery bag of eggshells and coffee grounds and other trash, flew out through the flames, and wound up back inside the house, under the couch, inside my comic book, closing the cover over itself on the way... Yeah, okay. No. I didn't buy it, not for a minute.

I felt a small twinge of panic creep up the back of my neck. As I stared at the evil look on the little boy's face in the picture, I knew I would have to take drastic measures. I decided I would burn the photograph. I'll remind you I was only six years old or so at the time, so the fact that, even being so young, I wanted rid of the photo so badly speaks volumes about how frightened I was regarding the creepy, teleporting photo.

As stated above, we burned our garbage at least once a week, and although I had never performed the task completely unsupervised, I had watched my dad often enough to know the drill. I took the photo and placed it in an empty Campbell's Soup can that I retrieved from the trash bags sitting in the garage, waiting to be burned. I snuck back in the house and "borrowed" a can of my mother's AquaNet hairspray, which I knew to be *extremely* flammable from a previous encounter with what was thought to be an empty can and the garbage pile (yes, I was lucky on several occasions that I didn't blow myself up or get severely burned). I sprayed the inside of the can with the photo in place until there was a quarter inch of hairspray in the bottom of the can.

I put the hairspray back (no one would ever be the wiser, hehe) and carried my little Molotov cocktail out to the garbage pile in the woods behind our house. It was in a huge bare spot and surrounded by a small U-shaped cinderblock enclosure, so there was little danger of fire spreading as long as it wasn't a windy day. I also clasped in my other little hand a box of "strike anywhere" matches. Yep, I was good to go. No evil demonic orphan kid in a photo was going to haunt me without a fight!

I gingerly placed the can at the edge of the charred remains of other garbage fires and began flicking lit matches in the general direction of the soup can from several feet away. After missing several times, I could no longer stand the anticipation—I walked right up to the can, struck a match with my trembling little hand and, once sure the flame had caught the matchstick well, flicked it in from about three inches. The next few mental images are vivid within my memory.

There was a whoosh and a resounding pop, as the walls of the soup can sort of acted as a tiny tennis ball cannon. I fell backwards, shielding my face from the gout of flame, which appeared to shoot two or three feet out of the can. Luckily, the can was leaning slightly away from me, or I would have gotten a face-full of the hairspray equivalent of napalm. The dripping flames started little fires throughout the garbage area, but quickly went out as the volatile fuel was consumed. And then, as if by magic, I saw the photograph on fire and wafting in the air. It fell near my feet, and I swear the dark, penetrating eyes of the boy were the last thing to burn. From the flaming can, I heard a weird noise, almost a knocking sound—I'm sure it was just the can buckling with the extreme heat—but in my mind, it was whatever was attached to the photo perishing in the fire. The knocking noise subsided as the fire burned itself out. When all that was left were cooling ashes and a few wisps of slowly curling smoke, I made my way back in. This time, I'm happy to report, the photo did not return to further vex me.

Years older now, I often wonder back on this event and try to figure out what all this was really about. The first thing that springs to mind is the story about the painting *The Crying Boy*. If you've never heard the story, be sure to Google it—it's worth a read and will make you carefully consider which thrift store find you bring home. I won't go into detail here, but *The Crying Boy* is a cursed painting or print that found its way into thousands of homes a couple of decades ago. A lot of the homes where it resides encounter tragedy (usually a fire, with the painting being the only thing that survives intact); therefore many people claim that there is a curse attached to the artwork. One of the stories is that the artist abused the boy in the painting so he would cry while being painted. It's a creepy story, no matter what the origin.

Was I dealing with something like that? An orphan

child who was able to place a curse on a photo that probably traveled into hundreds of homes in the 1960s US? Had I broken the curse by burning the weird photograph? If you've ever had an experience similar to this, by all means get ahold of me—my contact information, as always, can be found at the end of this book.

CHAPTER FIFTEEN

THE OAK RIDGE HOUSE

A couple of years after my daughter was born, her mother and I began renting a house in Oak Ridge. The house was right next door to my parents', so this made for ease of many things, including childcare. My parents simply doted on my daughter and wouldn't dream of allowing us to pay a stranger to care for her while her mother and I worked, so it was a matter of love and for the convenience of all involved. We hadn't been living in the house for very long when I began to sense something wasn't quite right.

For starters, the house was about as old as any in Oak Ridge, "the Atomic City" (also known as the "Secret City") for the part it played in the Manhattan Project during World War Two. In fact, my parents (like many Oak Ridgers) had met and married while working for the government in Oak Ridge, a city that, at the time, was behind a barbed and razor-wire fence and did not appear on any map. The US Army Corp of Engineers built all the houses in the 1940s. Because of the ongoing war and shortage of building materials, all of the houses were built with the back side facing the street. This saved on copper and lead piping, as all the hookups were foreshortened by turning the houses backwards. It was definitely an Oak Ridge thing that I never got fully used to, but you would walk into someone's house, entering through the kitchen door, walk through to the living room, and find a large plate-glass picture window looking out into the woods. That will mess with your head after a bit.

The house that we rented was one of four styles built by the USACE, this one being a three bedroom with a full finished basement. As I described earlier, the kitchen door faced the street, and the "front" of the house overlooked a small forest of trees in the backyard between the house and the houses on the other street behind.

The basement, while functional and utilitarian, was always a creepy affair. Myself, I would often take the basement stairs two or three at a time on the way up, because there was some presence or other down there that really made one feel unwelcome. There was also a rough hole high up in one cinderblock wall that provided access *underneath* the front porch. It wasn't unusual for houses built during this time (and during the height of the "Cold War" immediately following) to have some sort of "bomb shelter" in the basement, but I can't imagine the sheer terror of trying to ride out a bomb attack in that small, claustrophobic dirt-floored den, maybe twice the size of the largest dog house—all in all, I think I would have rather taken my chances with the bombs. Anyway, this hole was scary—something about it gave off a very strange vibe, and I kept it covered with many number of things, including cardboard, an area rug, posters, etc., because otherwise it felt like several sets of eyes were watching from within the darkened chamber.

The back corner of the basement was the worst. It felt as though there was constantly someone standing just out of sight in the shadows, or sometimes like someone had just left the area and you would feel a need to vacate the basement before they could return. One time, my teenage stepdaughter had a friend over who was an alleged psychic—she claimed to have sensed many spirits in the house, but claimed there were two dominant ones, in the form of an angry male spirit in the basement who hated all of us, and a shy female spirit in the attic who just wanted to be left alone. Odd as it sounds now, I think she was right on the money, based on experiences I and the whole household would come to experience.

One night, I was sitting in what would have been the dining room, where I had my computer equipment set up. Immediately to my right was a sliding glass door that led outside to the driveway. Directly in front of me and to the right was a wooden door that opened on a landing that allowed you to turn left and go down the basement stairs, or turn right and go out a single wooden door to the patio and driveway.

Everyone else was asleep when I heard the distinct sound of footsteps coming up the stairs from the basement. There were two small windows set way up high in the far basement wall, but other than that, the stairs were the only way in or out of the basement. No one had entered through the kitchen nor the outside door; otherwise I would have clearly heard them. The footfalls stopped at the top of the stairs, and I both heard and watched as the doorknob (which was locked from my side) slowly began to turn, repeating three times. I picked up a length of galvanized pipe, about five feet long, that we used to block the sliding glass door. I took aim like a baseball batter and threw open the door, ready to strike—but there was nothing there—nothing at all, although I had just heard and observed the knob trying to turn, and no footsteps had retreated down the steps, nor had the single, wooden door to the outside been opened. Everything was locked tight, and there were no lights on in the basement. I turned the lights on and slowly crept down the stairs, galvanized pipe still in hand —where I found the basement to be empty, silent and the windows locked from the inside, as expected. Stymied, I returned upstairs, double-checked all the locks, put the pipe in its place by the sliding glass door, shut off the computer, and went to bed. I didn't know what else to do—I was too unnerved to do any more computer work that evening and didn't want to sit there staring at the door, waiting for the locked knob to try to turn—so I called it a night and tried to go to sleep, although I distinctly remember tossing and turning for hours and jumping at each legitimate noise, such as the heat kicking on or water drip-drip-dripping in the bathroom sink.

Other times, I would observe small flashes of light, usually in the far end of the hallway where the bedrooms were located. I can think of no other way to describe this than to say it looked like the flashbulb for a camera, but shrunk down to the size of a pinprick. Later on, I found out that my now-grown daughter also used to frequently see these minuscule flashbulbs, as did her mother and half sister, who also lived in the house. Bear in mind that these were not near anything electrical—not even regular lights or electrical outlets. They would present themselves about two to three feet off the floor in front of a bare, painted wall with a bedroom door on either side. To my knowledge, as well as that of all the former occupants whom I have spoken with, this was the only location where the lights appeared. Sometimes they would just wink on and off, so quick that it was hard to see them unless you were staring directly down the hallway or managed to catch the flash in your peripheral vision. Other times, the lights would appear to flit and travel like fireflies—although the light was too small to be a "lightning bug," and the flash was a brilliant white rather than a greenish yellow glow one expects from the insect —plus these were visible all year round, day and night, very much unlike the common firefly.

Another common occurrence at the house was the sound of breaking glass. Sometimes, it would sound like something small, such as a tumbler or jelly glass had been dropped on the floor, shattering into pieces. Other times, there were loud crashes—loud enough that once I was sure that either the front picture window had been shattered, or perhaps the sliding glass door in the kitchen had slipped from the aluminum track and shattered. Another time, my daughter's mother and I had just put the baby down for a nap when we heard what sounded like the wooden door in the kitchen slamming hard enough to shatter the glass. It even awakened my daughter. However, in all instances, not a single shard of broken glass was ever found in any of the circumstances I have described above.

Breaking glass was not the only unexplained noise to be heard in the house. There was also the constant sound of footsteps, conveniently enough, wherever we *weren't*. For example, if we were in the kitchen or living room, we would hear what sounded like footsteps on the stairs or someone shuffling across the bare concrete floor in the basement.

If we happened to be in the basement, we would often hear the muffled footsteps of what sounded like small children racing up and down the carpeted hallway. It was also common to hear footsteps in the kitchen when we were downstairs. The sounds always ceased whenever we came up or went down, respectively, and the doors and windows were always found to be steadfastly locked and nothing disturbed or out of place.

It also was not unusual to hear things—objects—that weren't there. Once, while standing near the his and hers sinks in the bathroom, my daughter's mother and I heard what sounded like a handful of wadded plastic grocery bags being tossed into the closed shower stall, starting near the ceiling and uncompressing loudly as they continued to the tiled floor of the shower. Naturally, when I threw open the opaque glass doors, there was nothing to be found in the shower stall.

In the basement, we would often hear what sounded like someone dropping items from the ceiling and onto the floor. This ranged from what sounded like Ping-Pong balls to marbles to coins. The coins could sometimes even be heard to roll across the bare concrete floor before coming to rest—however, no Ping-Pong balls, marbles or coins were ever found on the basement floor, which only added to the mystery...

All in all, it seemed to be a peaceful coexistence that we had with whatever occupied our home. Things seemed to have more or less come to a complete stop, though, when a young pastor who was a friend of my brother visited the house. He claimed that there was demonic activity and blessed the house with anointed oil. In his words, there were "things that lived there, things that had been sent there, and things that had been attracted by the previous things." After his impromptu exorcism, no more strangeness was experienced, to my knowledge. We moved to a different house shortly after this, maybe a month or so, so I cannot attest to what may have occurred after we moved out.

The house still stands today, on the west end of Oak Ridge. Inasmuch, however, that this is a private residence and I do not know anything about the current tenants, I will refrain from revealing the exact address, and ask that anyone clever enough to deduce the location please respect the privacy of all involved.

CHAPTER SIXTEEN

THE CHRISTMAS FEATHER

[The odd thing about this tale is that it is not an entirely unique experience. In researching stories and reports for the second volume of More Strange Things in the Woods *(Lucky Secret Press, Bangor, Maine 2015), I came across another story eerily almost identical to my own personal experience. The other person's experience didn't happen outside, so it didn't make it into the book. I talk about it below, along with my personal experience.]*

When I was a child, our house in Solway had two living rooms. What we actually used as a living room had at once time been intended to be a dining room, but we instead ate at a small table in a nook off the kitchen. The room on the front of the house actually intended to be a living room was referred to by my parents (my mother in particular) as the "good living room." This meant that I was allowed to play, watch television, whatever, in the living room—but the "good" living room was off-limits—forbidden, verboten, no entry—this was reserved for entertaining or, in the Southern vernacular, "when we had company come over."

The only times when visitors weren't being entertained that it was permissible to be in the good living room was when I was doing homework and around the Christmas holiday season. The lighting was very good, which was why homework was okay to do in there. In regard to the holidays, the large picture windows across the front of the house, facing the street, were in that room and, as such, it was where we always placed our Christmas tree for maximum viewing pleasure. During such time as the room was decorated for Christmas, I liked to go and sit in the dark, the only light coming from the heavily decorated tree and accompanying windows. This was completely okay with my mother, as long as I didn't make a mess or put my feet up on any of the furniture. Sounded like a deal to me, and I spent many a winter's evening in the good living room, dreaming about what I might get in the way of Christmas presents. Life sure was good to a kid in the early 1970s—at least for this kid.

The first time I noticed the anomaly I came to refer to as "the Christmas Feather," I was probably about three to four years old. I can remember being in the good living room admiring the tree. My mother always insisted that we go all out for Christmas, and we always had a giant tree that, resplendent with a lighted star topper, almost brushed the ten-foot ceiling. Add in yards of garland, hundreds of winking, colored lights, dozens of blown-glass, hand-painted ornaments and dripping with faux icicles, and you get the idea of what the tree looked like—it was beautiful and a wonderful sight to behold—as a small child, it was not only a thing of beauty, but of magic and the joy that the season brought.

So, while lying on the couch enjoying the holiday spectacle of the tree, and an Andy Williams or Percy Faith or Perry Como Christmas album on the console stereo, I was basking in the glow of the seasonal magic. At one point, I happened to roll over on my back on the couch so that I could watch the reflections of the lights on the tree twinkle on the ceiling high above my head. Suddenly, I saw something hovering in my peripheral vision, just above me on the couch. I sat straight up and looked directly overhead, trying to get a better view. There above me was a lone gossamer feather, perhaps two inches long, pure white and very fragile and translucent. It didn't look at all like the robin or occasional crow feathers that I found sometimes in the yard.

I didn't know it at the time, but later in life I was able to verify that it was similar in appearance to goose down, although we never owned any down comforters or pillows or jackets or anything filled with feathers, due in part to my childhood allergies and also in part due to my mom's germophobia—when I did find those aforementioned robin or crow feathers, I was forbidden from bringing them into the house and would also receive a rather stern lecture about how birds carry disease, and there were such things as "bird mites," and the feathers were undoubtedly crawling with them and I should go and wash my hands immediately.

I watched the mysterious feather as it turned languid spirals in the air and seemed to float at random throughout the room. I would sometimes lose sight of it (the ceiling was painted a brilliant white as well), only to observe it pop up later in another corner of the room. I would also like to take the opportunity to state that we had no furnace, no central air and no fireplaces. Again, due to my allergies (I was particularly allergic to dust), when my father had commissioned the house built when I was six months old, he had insisted on the fairly modern concept (at that time in the early 1960s) of "ceiling heat," which worked via heated strips laid in the very sheetrock of the ceiling. While not very efficient, since heat moves upward by natural and physical law, it didn't cause any problems with my allergies. Also, being installed in the ceiling, it didn't create any "updrafts" associated with a furnace or forced-air heater, and therefore was *not* what was keeping my mystery feather aloft.

I can remember watching the feather for what seemed like hours. I was mesmerized by the aerial maneuvers and the way it would do things like circle the Christmas tree, as if it either possessed a mind of its own or was controlled by an unseen hand. I kept the feather as my own personal secret, lest my mother discover its existence and do away with it. Although there were times we were all in the good living room, including not only my parents, but my brother's wife and child when they came to visit, I never observed the feather unless I was the only one in the room.

There were a few instances where I boldly tried to catch the feather. I say "boldly," because it took a certain amount of boldness to climb on the back of the couch and assorted overstuffed, high-backed chairs to try to grab the feather, which seemed to always stay in the eight-to-ten-foot height range. My mother would have at least banned me from the good living room and at worst applied a hand swiftly to my backside had she witnessed such a transgression.

The oddest thing about the feather was that I only saw it around the holidays. Any other time when I was in the good living room, studying for example, the feather was nowhere to be found, no matter how long and hard I watched the ceiling waiting for it to appear. However, sometime after Thanksgiving, as soon as our decorations began to go up, the feather would return. I saw it during its yearly occurrence for several years, but —oddly enough—the feather seemed to have disappeared for good about the time I turned ten or eleven— in other words, as soon as I was big enough to have captured it.

Flash forward about forty years later. I have never forgotten about the feather and the mystery and awe I experienced, but I'm sure it was resting comfortably in the back of my mind—it was not the sort of thing I would sit and think about constantly, by any means. While collecting stories for my second book of true, weird tales—*More Strange Things in the Woods*—I had spoken with a gentleman about my age who had some unusual outdoor stories he wanted to tell. I recorded the stories and thanked him, and, as a matter of habit, asked if he'd had any other unusual experiences.

"There is one," he intoned solemnly, "but it didn't

happen in the woods, so I'm not sure you'd want to hear it."

I explained that even though it wouldn't fit within the scope of *this* book, I'd still love to hear any tale he wished to tell me. He began relating a story about—a Christmas feather. And a feather is what you could have knocked me over with as the story came pouring out, so similar to my own experience that it was frightening.

As he finished his story, he began to choke up a bit. He closed by stating that he believed with all his heart that the feather he encountered was the spirit of his deceased grandfather coming to wish him a happy holiday. He even claimed that his grandfather had told him as a child that when he passed, he would come back to him as a feather.

I thanked the man for his story, gathered my things and left. It was such a tender moment that there was no way I could blurt out, "Yeah, that happened to me too!" without a feeling of cheapening the moment when the man, really a stranger to me, had shared such a personal part of his childhood.

Although I have no idea how he felt about the afterlife—or feathers—my maternal grandfather passed away right after the holidays when I was just a few months old. "Could it be?" I have often asked myself after hearing the man's story. I can't say for sure, but I'm not one to rule anything out. If you know of a similar encounter, please write.

CHAPTER SEVENTEEN

THE PHANTOM MOTORCYCLIST

[This happened in west Knoxville, in an area of Ball Camp Road that was (at that time, in the early 1980s) heavily wooded farmland. The roads as well as the area have changed somewhat in the thirty plus years since this incident took place.]

I've told a similar version of this story on a couple of different radio shows, but I am telling it here for the first time in the print media (although I think I did post it on a blog somewhere, in a very short version, back in the 1990s, because I seem to remember someone asking for specific details because he lived in the area where it happened).

I was working at a fast-food restaurant in the Cedar Bluff area of Knoxville at the time. I had finished my shift, and as far as I can recall, it would have been sometime around midnight when I left the premises and got into my car. Instead of going home (I lived in Oak Ridge at the time, about fifteen miles away), I instead decided to stop by a friend's house. We were both night owls, and I knew that if his light was on, he would still be up and ready to chew the fat for a while.

On the way to the friend's house, I stopped by a Weigel's convenience store and put gas in my car (a beautiful old 1971 Chevrolet Impala, a giant green road boat of a car) and got some sodas and snacks to enjoy once I arrived at my friend's place.

As luck would have it, my friend's lights *weren't* on, so that meant he was still up and awake, just not at home. I was off the next couple of days and didn't have any particular place I had to be the next morning, nor any time I had to be there—so I played a little game I've played since I was old enough to drive, called "Chasing the Moon."

The concept behind chasing the moon is a simple one. There are only a couple of rules. The main rule is that you have a full tank of gas. The other rule is that you follow the moon—whenever you come to a crossroad or an intersection or any place where you have a choice in direction of travel, you defer to whatever direction the moon is in. Pretty simple, but loads of fun. I've discovered new places and been hopelessly lost—but I always had a great time doing it.

On that particular night, chasing the moon took me into some not totally unfamiliar territory, places I wouldn't normally drive without a purpose for sure, but that was kind of the point of this whole exercise, anyway. I did this for about an hour or so, then decided it was time to drive back by my friend's house and see if he was back at home yet.

He still wasn't back, I could see the bare parking spot he normally used, as I had approached from a different street this time, so I decided that this predicament called for more Chasing of the Moon, and off I went on another driving tangent. That was the reason I had approached his house from a different direction, so in case I ended up driving around more, I would head into different areas.

At some point, I found myself on a lonely stretch of Ball Camp Road, which in 1983 was still heavily lined with farmland (I haven't been back to visit in more than a dozen years as of this writing, so I'm sure it looks quite different now, what with the real estate boom in West Knoxville and all). As I tooled along, I just happened to glance up into my rearview mirror—and saw that a motorcycle—with no lights on at all, no less—was mere inches from my rear bumper. Thankfully, my first reflex wasn't to hit the brakes, but I did slow down. I assumed that the rider had encountered some sort of electrical problem with his motorcycle and was riding my bumper for safety. I would consider that a good plan, under those circumstances.

I knew there was a stop sign coming up ahead, and when I stopped, I would get out and see where the driver was headed. I could even offer to let him ride in front of me, or for that matter, my Impala was big enough we could have lashed the motor bike in the trunk and I could have safely driven him wherever he needed or wanted to go. I tried to catch his attention in the mirror as I rolled up on the stop, but he remained steadfast on the bike. I stopped the car, opened my door and stepped out—only to be greeted by nothing behind me. The motorcycle and rider that had been there mere seconds before was nowhere to be found. I listened for the telltale sound of a four-stroke engine, but heard nothing other than crickets and the low thrum-thrum-thrum of my idling Chevy. We hadn't passed any side streets, and I knew for sure that he hadn't passed me, so I assumed he had flipped a U-turn and headed back in the other direction. I climbed back in my car and continued on, towards the direction where I could make out the moon through the trees.

I had been driving again for a couple of minutes, puzzled by what had just taken place, when I glanced in my rearview mirror and did a double take—the motorcycle and rider were back—and still no lights on, none at all. Okay, now this was starting to freak me out. I tried speeding up; he remained about the same distance. I tried slowing down, the same results. At one point, I even stopped in the middle of the road and the bike stopped too, just in the edge of the light from my brake and taillights. I knew that if he were sitting that far behind me and another car came upon him, he'd be toast (I'm assuming it was a "he," as the body frame and shape appeared male, but with the helmet and black/dark clothing, I can't say one hundred percent). I rolled my window down and was shocked that there was no motorcycle engine to be heard. I was really feeling creeped out at this point, so I mashed the gas and took off as fast as I could safely (well, sort of) go...

The motorcycle kept up for a while, and I was seriously considering driving to the nearest police station. However, it was at this moment that an odd occurrence took place. I had just crossed a narrow bridge over a small creek... and boom—no more motorcycle. I took a few extra winds and turns, constantly checking my rearview mirror, but the phantom motorcyclist never returned. I went to my friend's house and found that he had subsequently arrived, and the lights were on. I went in and told him my tale, and by this time I had processed it enough to be shaken after the initial adrenaline faded away. He insisted that we get in his car—he'd drive while I navigated, and we'd try to retrace the route. We did this for an hour or two, yet never saw the phantom cyclist that night—or any other, ever.

Later on, I was reading a book of hauntings and ghostly encounters. One of the stories was about a certain pond in New England. It was said that just after you passed the pond, while on horseback, you would feel someone mount the horse behind you—presumably, according to legend, the ghost of a Revolutionary War soldier who had drowned in the pond after being shot by a Hessian soldier. The story continued that you would continue to feel the presence on the horse behind you until you crossed a covered wooden bridge; then the presence was gone—ghosts cannot cross moving water, the book had stated matter-of-factly.

I have often wondered—was I experiencing a modern-day version of this legend, of a sort? It makes for interesting thinking, nonetheless.

CHAPTER EIGHTEEN

GHOSTS OF THE BIJOU

[The Bijou Theater on Gay Street in Knoxville, Tennessee, is a beautiful old building dating back before the turn of the last century. Much like its larger counterpart across the street, the Tennessee Theater (which is also purported to be haunted, by the way), it harkens back to the day of the grand showplaces that existed before the blasé multiplex cinemas of today.]

For a beautiful old theater, the Bijou Theater (once also known as the Lamar House) in Knoxville sure has some bad vibes and occurrences. I had never really paid much attention to the theater and had only observed it while driving by, but after my initial experience and I began to delve into its history, I learned what a dark past the beautiful old building had accrued.

My first encounter at the Bijou was in 1989. A surgeon whom I worked for in Oak Ridge had just completed his law degree at the University of Tennessee

School of Law in Knoxville. Pleased upon graduating (attorneys who can boast and MD, JD after their names are cunningly rare), he took his entire office staff out to celebrate after the graduation ceremony. Due to its (somewhat) close proximity to the law school, the office manager from the surgical practice booked a private banquet room at the restaurant attached to the theater, known as the Bistro at the Bijou.

The Bistro offers very elegant dining to match the elegant interior of the attached theater, but I'll get back to that in a moment. In the meantime, let's look into the not-so-elegant history of Knoxville's Bijou Theater...

Originally the Lamar House Hotel was a place where Knoxville's wealthy and elite met in the Victorian era. Around 1909, it was decided that what the hotel needed was an auditorium, and what was to become known as the Bijou was built. It hosted many grand and famous performers of the day, including Dorothy Gish, John Phillip Sousa and even the Marx Brothers once graced the Bijou's stage. On any given night, 1,500 people could be found inside watching the second run of the latest Hollywood epic such as *Ben-Hur* (Knoxvillians watched first-run movies at the much larger and grander Tennessee Theater across the street, which opened in 1928), or traveling performers, such as famed magician Harry Blackstone, or the famous Ballet Russe with Anna Pavlova.

However, by the late 1960s and late 1970s, Knoxville's once vibrant downtown had deteriorated, and the Bijou had followed suit. Now, the blocks on South Gay Street where the elite and wealthy once met were lined with flophouses, heroin dens and houses of ill repute. The once grand Bijou barely remained open, and only did so because it was now showing pornographic movies.

In early 1974, the owner of the Bijou at the time was tossed out due to unpaid property taxes, and it looked like the entire building, including the now seedy Lamar House, would fall victim to the dreaded wrecking ball. However, a group of Knoxvillians with a fondness for architecture and a disdain for parking lots (many of Knoxville's elegant old turn-of-the-century buildings were leveled and inexplicably turned into parking lots—which didn't make any sense—"Downtown" Knoxville was dead and dying—the once "fancy" shops both on the promenade and surrounding historic Market Square were shuttered, boarded and empty—a once grand era of shopping had given way to strip malls in far-flung corners of Knox County as well as the 1.3-million-square-foot "mega mall" named West Town, which had opened on Kingston Pike in 1972, a mere few miles in a straight line from Knoxville's Downtown). The Bijou was saved and currently is a showcase for national touring entertainment acts (although I did witness the infamous Ramones perform a concert here back in the day).

But along with the elegant trappings, the Bijou harbors some leftover "residents," most of which are none too happy. From what I've read as well as personally experienced, the entire place is active with a number of ghosts, from the downstairs bathroom to the top floor, where a Confederate general, injured in the battle of nearby Fort Sanders in the Civil War, unfortunately passed away.

So, back to the story, here I was in the Bistro attached to the theater, eating and drinking on my employer's dime—the '80s were very good to me in that way. After washing down platefuls of hors d'oeuvres with a few glasses of expensive champagne, I found myself in desperate need of the gentlemen's facilities.

The Bistro was crowded (there were other parties of revelers besides ours) and I couldn't navigate a clear path to the restroom without disrupting a bunch of total strangers. So, knowing that the theater next door had restrooms, I hightailed it through the connecting doors and into the darkened edifice. Unbeknownst to me at that time, there was a set of restrooms RIGHT THERE in the lobby. Maybe it was the champagne or maybe it was spirits of another sort, but somehow I failed to see those restrooms (clearly marked, as I discovered on subsequent visits) and instead headed up the pitch-black stairs to the mezzanine level, where I knew there were restrooms.

Groping along in the dark, I made it about halfway up the staircase when I got an eerie feeling. Like I wasn't alone on the stairs. And when I say pitch-black, I'm not exaggerating—the stairway was totally blackout darkened. I slowed down, gingerly took a few more tentative steps, then decided this was probably a Very Bad Idea. Before I could turn and begin to make my way down, I felt a very light touch on my arm, like the fingers of a tender female. Every hair on my neck and arms stood up. It felt as though I'd been hit with a bolt of electricity. I don't think my feet touched the dozen or so steps I covered on the way down. I raced out the front door of the theater and trotted around the corner and into an alley on Cumberland Avenue, just behind the theater. Thankful I hadn't soiled myself during my escape, I did what anyone would do—I contentedly peed in the alley behind a dumpster.

Relieved, I ventured back into the Bistro, to be met with a large crowd coming out. It seemed all the other parties were leaving, so I went to another restroom in the restaurant that had been unavailable earlier to wash my hands, a consolation, at least. When I went back to my group's private room, I didn't mention my little foray, but did find that I was now 100% sober. Nothing kills a good champagne buzz like literally having the pee-water scared out of you. I heartily quaffed a few more glasses of Dom or Moët & Chandon or whatever expensive libation was being toted around on silver trays by the rather glum-looking waitstaff. I had to steel my nerves, you know, after such a frightening and harrowing experience. I could have soiled my trousers in front of my peers and co-workers, after all...

While comforting myself, I began to have doubts about what I had experienced. It was after midnight (the Bistro was staying open just for us, as my employer was well in his cups and had promised everyone working over at the restaurant a large tip), and I decided to have another go at the stairs out in the theater lobby. Good thing I wasn't drinking tequila, I suppose.

I strode out into the lobby, leaving the sounds of laughter and clinking glasses behind. As soon as the door closed, however, the theater lobby was silent as a tomb. I began creeping my way over to the stairs. There was a dim light in the theater, but after the first step or so, the stairs were still as dark as a dungeon. I slowly mounted the stairs, taking them slowly, one at a time. As I gingerly placed both feet on the third or fourth step—I heard voices.

I stood, frozen, and tried to figure out where the voices were coming from. I looked up the darkened stairway and realized (thankfully) that it wasn't from up there. I backed down the stairs and began retracing my steps, still hearing voices just out of earshot—I could hear them talking, but not really plain enough to know what was being said. There was one male voice and one female voice.

I suddenly realized that the voices were coming through the doors to my right, which would be the doors that led into the main seating area of the ground floor. The voices were a bit clearer, although I could still only pick out bits and pieces of what was being said. The more I listened, the more it became evident that the persons in question were rehearsing a play, as I heard what sounded like some of the same phrases being repeated.

Relieved, but curious, I stealthily grasped one of the massive door handles to peer in on the practicing thespians. I still heard the voices while my hand was on the handle, but as I silently eased the door open just a crack, the voices abruptly stopped. I found myself peering into a totally darkened theater. There was no rehearsal. There were no longer any voices. Once again, I beat a hasty retreat into the Bistro. This time I stayed put until it was time for my ride to take me home.

Years later, I was in the Bijou once again. It was near Halloween, and my wife at the time and stepkids had gone into downtown Knoxville for some spooky festivities. The Bijou wasn't part of the spooky event, but as we passed by it, I knew my wife and stepdaughter were looking for a place to use the restroom. I tried the door for the Bijou and, sure enough, the lobby was open.

Just to the right of the entryway were the restrooms I had mysteriously missed some ten years or so prior. I went into the men's and confirmed that the restrooms were quite old, done in almost art deco style reminiscent of the 1920s or '30s—obviously, they hadn't been installed in the last ten years, which I wanted to verify, just in case.

I finished my business rather quickly and waited outside the ladies' room next door. From inside the ladies' room, I kept hearing squeals, so I assumed my stepdaughter and her mother were goofing around and having fun. Shortly, the door was flung open and my stepdaughter came charging out, a look of sheer terror on her tear-streaked face. Her mother soon followed, looking not quite as scared but for sure perplexed.

"Let's get out of here," she breathed, glancing back over her shoulder toward the restroom. Her daughter had already burst through the main door and was dancing around spastically on the sidewalk, both hands over her mouth. After we hit the sidewalk, the girls took off in a fast trot—almost a run—and didn't slow down until we were several blocks farther up Gay Street, somewhere in the vicinity of the aforementioned Tennessee Theater.

Once I got them calmed down enough to explain what happened, I must say I wasn't that surprised, based on my own misadventures in the Bijou after dark. My wife, shaking, explained that while they were in the restroom doing what comes naturally, they'd heard voices talking. The voices, one male and one female (sound familiar yet?) seemed to be in the restroom with them. Her daughter had begun to panic, but my wife looked into every stall and confirmed that they were alone. About that time, the toilet in the stall next to them flushed. As my wife watched in horror, two of the sinks turned themselves on, sprayed a bit of water, then turned themselves off. The voices continued their litany just out of earshot (again, very similar to my experience, which the girls knew nothing of). So that was when we left.

If you search on YouTube, you can see video of a paranormal investigation team picking up some very clear "Class A" EVPs (EVP is short for electronic voice phenomenon, a process by which some people claim voices from the past can be recorded) in the Bijou. My best advice, if you're up to it, is to go check out the theater for yourself. You may just walk away a more firm believer than when you went in.

[The historic Bijou Theater (http://www.knoxbijou.com/) is located at 803 S. Gay St., Knoxville, TN 37902. The phone number is (865) 522-0832.]

CHAPTER NINETEEN

MISCELLANEA—A HODGEPODGE HAUNTED

[In this chapter, I have chosen to group together some otherwise unrelated incidents. While the experiences were fascinating to me, I didn't feel that any of these warranted a chapter devoted all to the singular incidents.]

THE BEWITCHED MIRROR

[Normally, when you look into a mirror, you see an exact opposite reflection. In other words, if you move your left hand, your mirrored reflection appears to move the right hand, and so on and so forth. But what if a mirror reflected just the opposite, in effect giving you the same view of yourself that everyone else sees? Well, now in the twenty-first century, the technology does

exist—while researching this entry, I found such a mirror. However, back in the mid-1970s, I encountered a mirror in an antique shop that gave me my reflection as everyone else would see me—over three decades before the technology existed.]

This is a short—but very weird—tale. I was in an antique shop with my parents, somewhere in East Tennessee, if memory serves correctly. The year would have been around 1972–73, making me about nine or ten years old. My parents were antique dealers themselves, with active booths in several area antique malls during the 1970s and 1980s. On any given weekend, we would visit a multitude of antique shops, junk stores, thrifts, garage sales, and auctions.

In this one particular shop, I was wandering around in the back of the store, not looking at anything in particular. We had been at this all day, and I was ready to get home and relax with a book or some television. Suddenly, something caught my eye. It was a very tall and ornately carved mirror. It was black and very "goth" looking, even at a time before such an aesthetic existed (I'm talking modern gothic here, not the ancient Goths and Visigoths). I stood looking over the strange carving in the black wood of the mirror and raised my hand to have a sip from the bottle of soda I was carrying. I noticed immediately that instead of seeing my reflection in the mirror, I was seeing the opposite. If I raised my right hand, I saw myself raise my right hand in the mirror, instead of my reflected left, as normal. In short, instead of seeing a backwards reflection, I was seeing myself exactly as other people would see me. I was amazed at the novelty of the mirror and stood in front of it making motions and silly faces until my parents called for me to leave. It wasn't until later in my teenage years that I realized that what I had witnessed in the mirror was absolutely impossible—at least under normal conditions, in what appeared to be an old, flat glass mirror with the edges of the silvering beginning to flake off.

I never saw the mirror again and remain unsure even which shop it had been in. I find it odd, thinking that somewhere out there, someone may have a dusty old mirror sitting in their garage—not just any old mirror, mind you—but a bewitched mirror that must have come straight from the *Night Gallery*.

THE BROWN MOUNTAIN LIGHTS

[The (in)famous and fabled Brown Mountain Lights of Western North Carolina have been written about in song and story for at least the last one hundred and fifty to two hundred years. When I lived for a short time in the extreme northeasternmost corner of Tennessee, I welcomed the opportunity to visit Brown Mountain on as many occasions as possible.]

The Brown Mountain Lights are one of those incredible things that you simply have to see for yourself in order to grasp just what is going on. And it's not like they're a rarity—countless thousands of people have observed them over the last several decades. There are well-known spots along the highway where the lights can be seen, particularly in the summertime, but I found the best viewing to be on the bluffs at Wiseman's View, overlooking Linville Gorge.

On the dozen or so trips I have made to Brown Mountain, the lights have never failed to appear. Maybe I just have exceptional luck or a lot of patience or both, but I've always left amazed, never disappointed.

The legends claim that the lights are the spirits of warring Indian tribes, forever left to battle back and forth in the mountains. Other legends state that it is the spirit of a woman searching in the mountains for her lost husband. There are other legends and stories, but those two seem to be the most often told variants.

Scientists from several universities have studied the phenomena of the lights, but only left with more questions and no solid answers. Some naysayers and skeptics have trotted out every possible explanation, from swamp gas, piezoelectricity, foxfire, or even the reflections of distant trains or automobiles—the last two explanations are particularly laughable, as stories of the lights have been told well prior to the advent of either trains or automobiles in the area.

My best advice is to witness it for yourself. Arrive early, before dark, and settle in. Be patient, it's worth the wait. Sometimes the lights appear above the trees, sometimes within them. Sometimes the lights are different colors; other times they appear to be a type of dim fluorescent—but if they are one thing at all, it is simply amazing.

[For more information, including photos, videos and detailed travel directions, visit http://www.brownmountainlights.com]

· · ·

THE HAUNTED MARTHA WASHINGTON INN

[The Martha Washington Inn in Abingdon, Virginia, has a remarkable (albeit somewhat checkered) past. Not only has it been host to a large number of celebrities and visiting dignitaries, it is believed to be one of the most haunted hotels in the United States.]

Abingdon, Virginia, is a sleepy little town. To visit there is like stepping back in time. It reminds one of the fictional "Mayberry," as depicted on television.

One of the highlights of Abingdon is the famous Barter Theater, located on the town's main drag. But across the street from the Barter is the world-famous Martha Washington Inn. It's been everything from a boarding school for wealthy turn-of-the-last-century girls, to a field hospital during the Civil War, to a morgue in the winter immediately following. The Martha Washington, by way of its expansive and rather dark history, has a history of being haunted.

From a violin-playing ghost to a bloodstain that continues to reappear, to an apparition that was seen on a security camera, there's a little haunting here for everyone.

During my several stays in the Martha Washington, I've stayed in several of the haunted rooms, including the bridal suite, room 403, room 217, and the room that contains a bed that reportedly belonged to Napoleon. My experiences here have run the gamut from disembodied whispering, a strange rapping on all the walls in a room in quick succession, and a smell I can only describe as the dirtiest wet dog you've ever smelled. The elderly concierge, who has worked at the hotel for decades, told me this wet-dog smell is often experienced in conjunction with the sighting of the ghost of a Civil War soldier.

If you ask around nicely, many of the employees of the hotel will tell you of some of the more frightening encounters, such as bloodcurdling screams and the time that all the paintings fell from the walls—and remained standing on their edge. If you're the least bit sensitive to the paranormal, be prepared to experience many things here, and try not to become overwhelmed.

[The Martha Washington Inn is located at 150 W Main St, Abingdon, VA 24210. Phone: (276) 628-3161 http://www.themartha.com]

CHAPTER TWENTY

IN CONCLUSION

Well, there you have it. These are not all of my stories, but at least they are what I feel to be the most interesting ones that I am willing to share. After a lifetime thus far spent in pursuit of the paranormal, the unexplained, the supernatural and the mysterious—I find that as I grow older, I have more questions than I do answers. I don't say this grudgingly; the fun is always in the pursuit. I would rather discover a thousand things I can't explain than to find a boring, plausible explanation for one singular something that was otherwise magical. Not to say that I'm not skeptical in regard to some things, I just prefer the things that leave even skeptics speechless and shaking their heads.

    I thank you for the time you invested in reading this book, and I look forward to greeting you amongst the pages of whatever book will be the next one published. As always, I enjoy hearing from my readers, whether you have a story to tell or are just stopping by to say "Howdy." All the contact information you could ever want is found at the end of this volume.

ABOUT THE AUTHOR

Steve Stockton grew up in the wilds of East Tennessee, but now makes his home in the Pacific Northwest, where he enjoys finding all kinds of new, weird places to seek out. As well as the great outdoors, he also enjoys hearing from his readers.

If you have a story you'd like to share for future volumes or would just like to say hello, you can reach him at SteveStockton81@Gmail.com

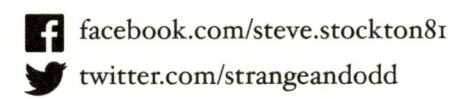

facebook.com/steve.stockton81
twitter.com/strangeandodd

ALSO BY STEVE STOCKTON

STRANGE THINGS IN THE WOODS

Milton Keynes UK
Ingram Content Group UK Ltd.
UKHW041435310723
426083UK00001B/6

9 781734 419825